Playing HIDE & SEEK

A Non-Churchgoer's Path to Finding God

Publisher's Note

Playing Hide & Seek is a book that is difficult for us to publish, yet we believe it must be published. There are millions of people for whom God is real in spite of a church that to them seems irrelevant and even destructive. Micheal Elliott's views speak for these persons and offer them guidance.

For those who love the church and seek to work through its ministries, this book is both perplexing and disturbing. In fact, none of the publicly known church leaders we contacted would endorse this book. Most, however, encouraged us to publish this book because it offers an enormously important word to the significant numbers of people who seek for God yet avoid the church.

We therefore offer *Playing Hide & Seek* for all those who search for God, both inside and outside the church.

Playing HIDE & SEEK

A Non-Churchgoer's Path to Finding God

MICHEAL ELLIOTT

PEAKE ROAD

Macon, Georgia

ISBN 1-57312-057-X

Playing Hide-and-Seek
A Nonchurchgoer's Path to Finding God

Micheal Elliott

Copyright © 1996
Peake Road

6316 Peake Road
Macon, Georgia 31210-3960
1-800-747-3016

Peake Road
is an imprint of
Smyth & Helwys Publishing, Inc.®

Library of Congress Cataloging-in-Publication Data

Elliott, Micheal, 1956–
    Playing hide-and-seek:
    a nonchurchgoer's path to finding God/
    Micheal Elliott.
    x + 102 pp.   6" x 9" (15 x 23 cm.)
    Includes bibliographical references.
    ISBN 1-57312-057-X (alk. paper)
    1. Spiritual life—Christianity. 2. Desire for God. I. Title.
    BV4501.2.E375   1996
    248.4—dc20   96-14321
                                                      CIP

Contents

We have been so brainwashed, so victimized, so conditioned by the organized, institutionalized churches; and we equate the Christian faith with these most evil of all institutions, those high spires, and stained glass, and big bells, and silver chalices, and parking lots, and Betty Crocker kitchens for the sacrament of coffee hours.

—Will D. Campbell

The perfect worship service is one in which we are so completely unaware of what is taking place around us because we are so in tune with the presence of God.

—C. S. Lewis

Preface

Before you move ahead and start reading this, let me take a moment to tell you a few things. I believe in God, but I'm not certain what all that means anymore. You would think someone with a divinity degree would not say such a thing. Oh, I know a lot about what other people have said about God. Then we have church history, comparative religions, theology, church management, and a lot of other things that have very little, if anything, to do with God.

One day I was driving back from lunch with some friends and was suddenly struck by the fact that, in spite of intense training on the subject, I was still looking for God then as much as I had before seminary. Many members of the clergy do not want to admit this, for it would be like a brain surgeon who is preparing to operate on us blurting out that she hopes she can locate the problem. It is this way with the clergy. Most are always trying to project an image of complete confidence on the subject of God, but they don't really have any better idea than anyone else where God is.

So I got to thinking about the things I have done to look for God in my life and tried to learn whatever lessons there were from the experiences. First, I noticed that religion often has very little to do with God. I also discovered that most of my own searching had centered around various expressions of religion but had little, if anything, to do with God. Religion, it seems, is our attempt to make something tangible out of something not so easily discernible. What you will read are some of the lessons I learned from my own game of hide-and-seek with God.

Every year or so someone produces a study claiming that most people believe in God, although a substantially less number are active in their attendance at a church or synagogue. I think this is one of the ways we are saying that religion has had very little to do with finding God in our lives. Religion often leaves us frustrated and wanting, but this does not seem to get in the way of our intense desire to experience God. Because of this, you will read some experiences from the hide-and-seek game of faith. It is really nothing more than that, except the game of hide-and-seek involves finding —and finding the God we believe in is what it's all about.

There are a few folks I would like to thank, because one of the things I don't do enough of is express the joy I feel over them.

—The Inklings, Many Ann Beil, Bill Broker, and Susan Watts, were the ones who helped me understand that I have been playing hide-and-seek all along.

—The Union Mission Board of Directors, especially Carole Beason, Debra Brook, Joe Daniel, Larry Harrington, Richard Moore, Elizabeth Sprague, Elmo Weeks, Ann Rockwell, Sharon Galin, Harold Yellin, Rabbi Saul Rubin, Louis Parent, James Piette, Jerry Robinson, Thomas Woodyard, and Frank Wooten, provide a wonderful place to be base when playing hide-and-seek.

—I have thanked the Union Mission staff, my family away from home, before, but I hope to convey how much each of them means to me. Julie Walsh, Joe Bridges, Alisa Monfalcone, Lynda Allen, Alloceia Hall, Lavanada Brown, Donald German, Iris Farmer, Jim LaBon, and Jennifer Beaufait are new additions to this family, and I appreciate all they do.

—Leslie Quarterman and Dianne Fuller were the first ones to read what I wrote, and I very much appreciate their encouragement.

—Annette Daniel spent hours on the grammar in the manuscript.

—Janice has always supported my attempts to figure out my sense of calling and allowed me the freedom to play hide-and-seek when I needed to.

—My children have helped me to think about many of the ideas here in their own unique ways, and I hope I have not dragged their intellect down to my level.

—Old friends and new friends have continued to make the word "friend" meaningful to me, and both have helped me to remember real love during a bad time.

—Two friends, Jodee and Cheryl Sadowski, owners of the World Famous Breakfast Club, have allowed me to have a wonderful setting to live out my convictions when I needed it the most.

As I was writing this book, my grandfather, Reverend Ira V. Carver, was very sick and confined to his bed at home. This confinement was very difficult following a lifetime of activity in which he gave his life to searching for God and helping others learn to play the game. His mind continued to travel, however, and he would describe for us where he had been that day. My grandmother, Edith Carver, spent the better part of a year taking care of him with assistance from their daughter Ann, eight other children, and numerous grandchildren and great-grandchildren. Most days, while confined to his bed, he would travel through space and time, back to his childhood or to another city where he had to accomplish some important task. Upon his return, he would tell us about his journeys. After months of such journeys, I have come to believe that he was just practicing for the trip to the other side. In the hide-and-seek game of faith, I think my grandfather found God, and now he won't let go.

To Rev. Ira and Mrs. Edith Carver

Chapter 1

Playing Hide-and-Seek with God

I think God likes to play hide-and-seek. At least, most people must think God likes the game. Preachers are forever talking about seeking God, so God must be hiding. Jesus even said "Seek first the kingdom of heaven," and if you're supposed to find it, then it must be hidden somewhere.

Everyone has played the children's game where someone closes their eyes, counts to ten, and then goes off searching for everyone hiding. It's always fun if you find who you're looking for, but it's very frustrating if you spend half an hour looking for someone so well hidden that, without any hints, they can't be found. A lot of games have ended with the searcher giving up and going home without ever telling the hidden ones the game was over. They continue to hide, of course, and hours later begin to realize no one is looking for them anymore. When they come out of hiding, no one sees them, and they go home. Everyone ends up frustrated.

I think it's this way with God. God is always playing the game. God hides, and we seek if we want to. We close our eyes, but, instead of counting to ten, we pray. After we open our eyes, we begin to look. Prayer is little more than telling God we want to play. The game begins when we start looking, and, like most children, we begin our search in all the wrong places.

Church, for instance, is one of the very first places people go when they're looking for God. It makes some sense to begin looking for God here because so many people claim that God is in a particular church. Upon entering, our first impression is that church is the type of place where God would likely hide. The buildings are full of crosses and pictures of God. The minister is telling everyone who enters they can find God here. The music is supposed to be the kind God likes. Thick carpet, pipe organs, offering plates, and heavy tables inscribed with the words "Do this in remembrance of me" are evidently the kinds of furnishings God prefers. Stained glass windows depict scenes of other people who played the game and found God.

The other people in church are filled with anticipation that they will find God, and this is contagious. Our own sense of expectation rises, and our search becomes intense. The service proclaims God is here, and we want to believe it so much we convince ourselves that God must indeed be present. After a while, though, we begin to feel like the child who has spent a long time looking for someone she can't find. We give up and go home. I think God very rarely hides in church, and people who look there are very dedicated to the game, refusing to give up. In many ways, church is a support group of people forever playing the game but rarely succeeding.

The Bible is another place where people look for God. Although I have never met anyone who has been able to success-fully hide in a book, God is supposed to be omnipresent—which means God can hide most anywhere. We grab the book and spend countless hours reading about prophets and apostles, Israel and law, wars and devils, and even Jesus playing the game by seeking out the lost. Some people claim to be very inspired by all of this, but no one finds God when they shut themselves up and read a book. Remember, the Bible is a book about God; it is not God. At worst, it is a collection of stories about some other people who found God when playing the game. At best, it is an instruction manual for how to play the game.

After years of seeking God, I have made up my own list of rules for playing hide-and-seek with God. It is not exhaustive, as I am forever adding to it. Several rulees have remained on the list for quite some time now, and I believe they are helpful when looking for God.

Some Rules for Playing Hide-and-Seek with God

- God is very rarely hiding where we think.
- Playing hide-and-seek with God is almost always a small game; just you and God are playing.
- When God comes out of hiding, it is very rarely what we expect, and we fail to recognize that we have found God.
- People often stop looking too soon.
- God rarely attends church. When God does go to church, congregations do strange things.
- God likes to surprise people when coming out of hiding and is often very unconventional in the presentation.
- After someone finds God, they are forever changed.
- After finding God, one becomes a storyteller.
- After someone finds God, they want others to find God too.
- People who have found God never stop playing the game, although many make the mistake of thinking they will always be able to find God in the same place.

Anyone who has played knows that the game may become a bit desperate, especially if our mothers are calling us to come home for supper or it's getting dark. After searching in the places where we think God would be, we start looking at everything in a frantic attempt to find God. Staring at the nighttime sky, we see if the man in the moon is really God. The ocean would make an excellent hiding place, so we may walk along the shoreline hoping to catch a peek of God coming up for air. Mountaintops seem to be places God would like, so we hike up one after another thinking the fresh air will clear our vision. Pilgrimages to holy lands and ancient shrines prove to be as useful as empty tombs when looking for God.

At this point many folks decide the game is not worth the effort and quit looking. Some announce they are agnostic about the whole affair and say they didn't really know what they were looking for anyway. Others claim to be atheist and argue there is really nothing to look for. Many still play hide-and-seek with God, but cease looking and begin focusing on others who claim to have found God. They believe if they surround themselves with people who claim to have succeeded, then their own chances of discovery are bound to increase. Attaching themselves to a charismatic storyteller, they hear all about God and how other people have been affected upon successfully completing the game.

Some of these charismatic figures are quite sincere in telling their story, backing up all their talk with enough action to convince those who are looking for God that they must have experienced something worth pursuing. The majority of these alluring leaders are all talk, however; but they talk so well to an audience desperately wishing to be convinced that they are perceived as godly substitutes for God. Besides, all these other people seem to think that hanging around charismatic talkers is as good as it gets, so they become faithful to the gatherings and lessen their commitment to playing hide-and-seek.

There are sometimes experiences of ecstasy when large groups of current and former God-seekers gather together in one place. Often, these gatherings resemble huge pep rallies in which people are encouraged to keep looking or are patted on the back for looking as long as they have. Sometimes a few in the crowd tell stories of their encounters with God, and these prove to be so powerful that the collection of people find God vicariously because they identify with the story and search. Unfortunately, these experiences are short-lived, and usually in a matter of hours the seekers are back to playing hide-and-seek alone

Of all the ones who begin playing hide-and-seek with God, only a few persevere with the game, refusing to become sidetracked. Those who do turn their attention to looking for God by devoting all their time to church, nature, or some religious leader often turn the game around—although they don't realize it. When they quit seeking God because they are seeking something else, God begins searching for them. They fail to realize they are now playing the game in reverse. It is now God who is looking for them. When found, they don't realize it is God who has discovered them because their attention was somewhere else. It gets to the point that God finds someone who refuses to acknowledge they have been discovered. Rather than coming out and playing with God, they close their eyes and play an imaginary game in the solitude of their hiding place.

Such a thing most often happens in church. Gathering with our support group of frustrated hide-and-seek-playing peers, we focus on a great many things associated with God and are too busy to notice when God actually attends. This brings up an important point about playing hide-and-seek with God. It seems God very rarely attends church. This makes sense, of course, since God is not particularly needed in church. When congregations gather together, it is for other purposes. Church is for singing, praying, storytelling, and some safety-in-numbers security—each to remind us we are still playing the right game. It is for mutual support and encouragement. It is a pooling of resources to help the poor and the downtrodden. It is a series of building committee meetings, fund development activity, choir practice, Sunday School classes, and trustee meetings. In short, church is a hotbed of activity that distracts one from actually looking for God.

Church is not the best place to have a personal, one-on-one experience of finding God, although on occasion God does indeed attend. Of course, no one is ever prepared for God actually attending church (otherwise it would be listed in the order of service prepared in advance), and congregations begin to do strange things when God actually shows up. With God in attendance, there is an outpouring of love, honesty, chastisement, and resolve to accomplish something. Everyone knows in no uncertain terms they are completely loved by everyone else who is present at the time (even the trustee who voted against what you wanted or the smelly stranger sitting in the back). Such an outpouring of love and acceptance leads to complete honesty in which people take off their masks and are content with being who they are without pretending to be someone else. There is an emptying of false pretensions and anything fake. Such honesty quickly leads to chaos, and everyone challenges everyone else to be better. Eventually, the confusion of such confrontation subsides, and each of the warring factions of the body of Christ is re-"membered." When God attends church, congregations become communities; and because very few congregations remain communities, we know that God rarely attends church.

More often than not, God is found outside formal religious meetings. It is difficult keeping up because, after all, God is God and can show up anywhere and at any time. In fact, there are several places where people have been very unsuccessful in finding God.

Unlikely Places for Finding God

• political conventions or rallies
• the White House, Congress, governors' mansions, city halls, or other meetings of politicians
• most for-profit hospitals
• most corporate board offices
• welfare offices (although God very often waits outside the door and accompanies people who are leaving)
• the pastor's study during sermon preparation
• finance committee meetings
• seminaries
• most places of entertainment

This is not to say that God never chooses to frequent these places. The likelihood of finding God in them is quite small, however. Too many other things distract from the game. It is very hard to play hide-and-seek while we're busy with a thousand other things. A successful game of hide-and-seek takes a great deal of dedication and concentration. Studying for a test, preparing a paper, making a profit, watching television, or winning votes distract from the game. God may indeed be waiting to be discovered in a corporate board office, but the business at hand prevents us from bothering to look.

Well, if God is not particularly fond of hiding in these places, where are the best places to look when playing hide-and-seek? There are a few good places to begin a search. A good place to look is Alcoholics Anonymous meetings. Across the country, in basements, social halls, and clubhouses, groups of men and women gather because of a common addiction. There is no other agenda than sharing the personal stories of one's addiction and some safety-in-numbers resolve to stay sober. They are not concerned about buildings, budgets, or agendas. One after another, individuals tell the stories of their pain. Somehow, healing takes place for those who stick with it long enough, and those gathered admit their need for a higher power.

I believe this higher power is one of the names God uses when playing hide-and-seek. People who go to A.A. can become so focused upon finding whatever will save them from their addictions that they refuse to acknowledge the possibility of not being helped. Then suddenly it happens. The higher power comes out of hiding, and recovery begins. Community breaks out. The higher power is revealed as God. It doesn't always happen this way, but more often than not, it does for those who continue to focus on what they are seeking.

God also hangs around the poor. There is no glamour in poverty, and those who work with the impoverished, the homeless, and the destitute are no better than anyone else (in fact, they are worse off). But God seems to have special affection for the poor. Because they have so little else to rely on, when the chips are especially down and there is no chance of making the rent payment, purchasing the groceries for an empty pantry, or getting the medicine, they call upon God. In spite of all odds, God comes through. Just enough money is found to keep the landlord happy for one more month. A soup kitchen provides the food that is not in the kitchen. A clinic dispenses the medication to sway the illness. Because of all the paperwork required and the tired and overworked administrators, however, the ordeal of receiving the assistance is almost as unbearable as the problem that brought the poor in search of help. By the time their needs are met, most are far too exhausted from the waiting on pins and needles for hours on end to notice the holiness of the act.

God is almost always present when the homeless are housed, the hungry are fed, or the sick are cared for; but the ones giving the help are normally too tired to notice, and the ones receiving are too exhausted from asking to realize it. I believe God respects the free-will giving and receiving taking place and stays in the shadows of the room, very close by but not in the way. If someone knows what they are looking for, they can see God during these times. It is often a funny sort of victory in the hide-and-seek game, though. A volunteer at a homeless shelter tells a mother and her two children that the shelter has no more room. As the weeping mother walks away with her frightened and bewildered children, the volunteer could swear it is God walking away with them.

There are other happier occasions when God comes out of hiding. God likes to participate in community building exercises, for example. There are many types of community building, and some are even in church settings. Well-read, middle-class people join together for marriage enrichment classes, divorce recovery workshops, men's groups, women's groups, race relations sessions, or with a special interest in achieving community. God must like it when people engage in self-discovery and such sharing, because many people participating in such activities seem to find what they are looking for and attribute it to God. Usually not knowing what to expect, many are striking out on an adventure, hoping they will discover something new about themselves or resolve some issue long bottled up inside.

As the group members get about the business of their agenda, however, they collectively begin to focus on one another. Someone tells a story, and others zero in on the story. A tug is felt as the story concludes, and someone follows with their own history. The group collects its own oral history, and each story becomes more personal and, often, more painful. A tear falls on someone's face as they begin to tell their story for the first time to a group of people intent upon hearing it. Story after story is told. History after history is revealed. Secrets are shared for the first time. Understanding is communicated and received. Everyone feels free to be themselves as individuals. They no longer pretend. They drop the masks they wore into the room. They are as they were created, without the inhibitions family and friends have placed upon them. When they leave, it is with a story to tell, one that is often repeated. These stories almost always are about finding God.

Sometimes, too, God simply likes to pop out of hiding and surprise us. We may not even know we are playing the game at the time. We are preoccupied with problems at the job, and we're trying to learn the new system when the old one worked fine. There is no time to play hide-and-seek with God when the boss is screaming about a deadline or one of the kids is having trouble at school and seems to be hanging around the wrong crowd. It is difficult to think about God when we're worried about our children. All kinds of important things distract us from looking for God. Then it happens. When we are least expecting it, God appears. An undeserved kindness is bestowed upon us when we do not deserve it. We mutter, "Thank God" because we cannot think of anyone else to thank. Deadlines are extended. Children turn out fine. The illness subsides. When everything has been going so wrong, something suddenly goes right. We are so thankful for it. We swear it must have been God darting by to remind us the game of hide-and-seek is never over.

Playing hide-and-seek with God can be very frustrating. Obviously, God is quite good at hiding, and we are not all that great at seeking. If it were up to us, the game would be called hide, seek, *and find.* It is not all that fun a game when we're forever seeking God and never able to do the finding. Like children, we quit and go home. It is probably because, as adults, we have forgotten that some games can take a long time to complete. Some even take a lifetime.

The other thing that complicates our seeking God is the fact that we think we know what we are searching. Many of us have convinced ourselves that when we find God, lightning flashes, thunder crashes, and the experience is so profound there is no doubt we have found God. Certainly we feel this way because too many others have told us this is what finding God would be like. We would all become like Moses upon seeing God, even the backside, and our faces would shine like a thousand suns. Or we might simply hear a voice like Paul on the road to Damascus, drop to the ground, and carry on a conversation. Then again, it could be like John described when he was stuck on the island of Patmos for all those years: God will come riding out of the sky wielding a sword and scaring the daylights out of anyone who sees it.

Certainly God can do these things, but there are scores of other ways to come out of hiding. Much more subtle appearances are in line with the still, small voice described by Elijah. It could be that we should be looking down instead of up when playing hide-and-seek with God. Many of us get frustrated when we are looking for

God because we have too many preconceived notions of what we are seeking. Remember, God is very rarely hiding where we think, and is often hiding where we don't think.

Places to See Unexpected Glimpses of God

• Wherever children are playing, God is close by.
• When we pass a hitchhiker on the road, God is close by.
• When barriers that separate people are torn down, God is close by.
• When someone forgives someone else, God is close by.
• When someone cleans up another's mess, God is close by.
• God attends all births.
• God attends most funerals.
• God likes it when people laugh and will almost always stop by to see what is so funny.
• God likes it when people share, and always affirms it.
• God likes a good story and will usually stop in to listen when a really good one is told.

Hide-and-seek is a funny game. It is no fun unless it is hide, seek, *and* find. It is so easy to get mad and quit playing when no finding is involved. Too many people have forgotten that the best places to hide are the last places we would think to look. Once we learn where all the good hiding places are, then the finding part of the game will become easy enough. So what are you waiting for? It's time to play.

Chapter 2
When God Is "It"

Nobody likes to be "It." Whenever kids play hide-and-seek, everybody wants to hide. It is always more fun to hide than to be responsible for the finding part. Whoever is "It" has to do the majority of the work, and there is always the possibility they will fail to find what they are looking for. No one likes to take such risks, so when choosing who will be "It," we cross our fingers and pray that someone else will be chosen. The same is true when playing hide-and-seek with God. We always want God to be "It." It is so much simpler and easier for us when God is "It." Besides, God is God; God should be "It." We get tired of doing all the searching all the time.

Sometimes God does choose to be "It" and comes looking for us. This is the way most of us like to think because it is more comforting believing God is in control of everything, including the search for the lost. It is always easier to be found than it is to find someone who is hiding—and we certainly like it when our religion is easy. Besides, there are so many other reasons we believe God is "It."

Ministers have said for years that we are lost and that God wants to find us. They cite numerous passages from the Bible about lost sheep, lost coins, and lost people; so we must be lost too, and God wants us found. They say God is always on the lookout for us, and when we want to be found, then we are. We are only found, however, when we want to be.

The hymnals we use in churches have songs such as "Pass Me Not O' Gentle Savior" and "Amazing Grace" (I once was lost, but now am found) that indicate we are lost and God is looking for us.

Most people learn their theology from the hymnbook because they sing the words but fall asleep during the minister's sermon.

We believe God is too grown-up to hide when playing hide-and-seek. This would mean that God acts childish on occasion, and this is too hard to accept. Grown-ups are always looking for their children who are forever hiding, and we are supposed to be the children of God, so it must be that way with us too. God is supposed to be the parent.

We all have had those occasions when, sitting in a church pew or alone over a cup of coffee, we ask God to come to us. Then we wait and hope against hope that something happens. This is another indication of how we believe ourselves to be the ones in need of being found and God to be the one to do the finding. Besides, at times we have gone off looking for God in church or at a retreat, but have not been successful in our searches. We conclude that God will have to be "It" because we have done our time doing the searching and have given up. If the game is hide-and-seek, then God *must* be "It."

We have all heard other people tell stories about how God found them. We conclude that if God found them, then God will find us in the same way. There are great stories about how God came to someone sleeping under a bridge or to someone out at sea in a horrible storm. *Guidepost* magazine is full of these stories each month, and they make great reading. Professional athletes find God in a lonely hotel room when they realize the millions of dollars they make will not make them happy. Housewives find God when their children go to college and join some cult. Men on exotic fishing trips find God when their raft explodes and they have to sleep outside for several days. Someone finds himself driving a runaway truck, and God appears to steady his hands on the wheel. But this kind of stuff never seems to happen to us. We are not professional athletes, don't know anyone in a cult, have never taken exotic fishing trips, and have not sat behind the wheel of a big truck.

The Bible is also full of great stories about people who were found by God. Abram was sitting around one day when God showed up and invited him to take a long walk. Moses was busy looking after a bunch of sheep when a bush caught on fire and talked to him. Paul was riding a donkey on the Damascus Road when God knocked him to the ground and issued new marching orders. Only we have the same problem as those persons in *Guidepost;* this stuff never seems to happen to us. God has never said go there, our bushes don't talk to us, and we are pretty certain that the last time we fell to the ground it was not God who pushed us down.

Finally, we have been taught that God is always with us. If this is true, then why do we have such a hard time seeing God? If God were with us all the time, we would certainly know it. After all, everybody knows what God looks like. Everyone knows God is either a bright light that talks or a very large, kindly old man wearing a white robe. The problem is not with us, because we know what God is supposed to do. The problem is God doesn't always appear to know how we want it done. If we had our way, God would subscribe certain rules when being "It" in hide-and-seek.

Rules We Wish God Would Observe

- God should find us when we want to be found (and leave us alone when we don't).
- God should always look like God, so we will not be surprised. (God should be as bright as a million suns or something very dramatic, so there is no mistaking the appearance).
- God should never be subtle when approaching us. (We want to be knocked off our foundation in the same way Paul was on the Damascus Road.)
- God should always be accompanied by thunder, lightning, and choirs of angels singing the *Messiah.*
- God should always say something very profound so that some of our great questions are answered on the spot.
- God should always show up to make us feel better whenever we want.
- God should heal sick people more often.
- God should perform more miracles, because most of us have never seen any big ones—and we would really like to.
- God should be willing to tell us the lottery numbers in advance every once in a while.

• If God would like to send angels, that is o.k., but they should follow all the above rules.

If God followed these simple rules, we never would have any problem in the hide-and-seek game of faith. We would get what we expected and know without doubt that we were getting God. Things would be so much easier—no doubt about God's existence, none of this denominational bickering, and only one true religion. Everyone would believe the same thing in the same way. It makes sense for God to be "It" this way. The problem is God doesn't play by these rules.

Therefore, many of us feel that it is not God doing the looking but ourselves. We go to church, mumble prayers of desire, or even watch television preachers in some attempt to find the God we want to find us. We end up frustrated or impassive about our religion. We conclude that if God wants us, then God knows where we are. God can simply find us, and, in the meantime, we get on with our lives.

Then someone makes the claim that God found them, and we are shocked anew into wanting to be found also. "Come on God," we plead, "and get down here with me!" Of course, the response is almost always silence. Why is God so quiet? Some begin to wonder if there is a God at all. Others resolve to double their efforts and fill their lives with activities they feel God approves. We attend church any time the doors are opened. We work with the poor, the sick, or the abused. We watch hour after hour of television preachers and even choose to send them money to the address flashed on the screen. We read hundreds of books about God. We lock ourselves up and pray without ceasing. We sing, holler, stomp our feet, and do all kinds of things to get God's attention. We do all this with some conviction that if we do enough, God will certainly reward us with a visit. Then we are either unconcerned or too busy to notice when God does pass by. We are still uncertain what we should expect when God visits.

Frederick Buechner wrote, "God cannot be expressed but only experienced."[1] We are all trying to define what we want that experience to be in our lives. We want the dramatic, the miraculous, and the extraordinary. God is great and all powerful; therefore, encounters with God should be fantastic experiences. But when the extraordinary does not occur, we feel let down and think we have not experienced God. Why would God choose humdrum, mundane, and normal everyday ways when making a divine encounter? We do not want a "still, small voice." We demand a massive invasion of angels!

In the hide-and-seek game of faith, God is "It" as often as we are, but we fail to connect, to find one another, because we are forever looking for something that God is not. God's expressions do not conform to our stereotypes. If God is indeed always with us, then the problem must be that we choose to remain ignorant of how God prefers to make a revelation. What do these encounters look like? In Buechner's novel *The Final Beast,* a young minister finds himself alone. He desperately wants to find God. Lying on the ground, he begins his search.

> "Please," he whispered. Still flat on his back, he stretched out his fists as far as they could reach—"Please . . ." then opened them, palm up, and held them up as he watched for something, for the air to cleave, fold back like a tent flap, to let a splendor through. "Please come," he said, then "Jesus," swallowing, half blind with the sun in his eyes as he raised his head to look . . .
> Two apple branches struck against each other with the limber crack of the wood on wood. That was all—a tick-tock rattle of branches—but then a fierce lurch of excitement at what was only daybreak, only the smell of summer coming, only starting back again for home, but oh Jesus, he thought, with a great lump in his throat and a crazy grin, it was an agony of gladness and a beauty falling wild and soft like the rain. Just clack-clack, but praise Him, he thought. Praise Him. Maybe all his journeying, he thought, had been only to bring him to *hear* two branches hit each other twice like that, to see nothing cross the threshold but to see the threshold, to hear the dry clack-clack of the world's tongue at the approach of splendor.[2]

When God is "It," we know we have been found because the experience is personal and simple, unassuming and quiet, intense and hushed. God obviously doesn't feel the need to impress anyone and enjoys the very personal encounter of a friend sharing a secret.

There is no need for a great presentation. After all, God is supposed to be like a loving parent who plainly wants to be with us, not an egotistical monarch with the need to always make a grand impression.

We know God is often "It" in our hide-and-seek games. We spend too much energy defining how we want God to be "It." As a result, we miss all the ways God tags us, letting us know we have been found. There are all kinds of ways God tags us, but we fail to recognize it is God. We are looking for splendor, while God is comfortable with simplicity.

What to Look for When God Tags Us

- God can tag us anywhere, although we must be very focused on God and have a sense of expectation.
- God's touch is always a simple and very light personal connection. Even if we are in a crowd, it is a very personal experience.
- We do not necessarily see or hear anything out of the ordinary, but we feel something and have no doubt it is God.
- God's touch lingers for a while; and during this time we feel a sense of detachment from ourselves, a contentment with our surroundings, and a strong sense of compassion for those around us.
- We find it very difficult to describe the feeling of experiencing God to someone else, but we are motivated to try anyway.
- God's touch almost always moves us to a new sense of wonder and appreciation of our world and the people we know.
- We can always conjure up the memory of God's touch, and the recollection is physical.
- After we are touched by God, we always want to repeat the experience.
- After we are touched by God, we are moved to try new things.
- After we are touched by God, we feel at peace with ourselves.

Such experiences are not what we necessarily want, but they are always what we need. First, we must want to be found. Second, we must get ourselves to the point where we can recognize what it feels like to be found without heaping a ton of unrealistic expectations upon the experience. Once we have moved ourselves to the point of being found, then we may be found.

Robert Fulghum put it this way:

> Did you ever have a kid in your neighborhood who always hid so good, nobody could find him? We did. After a while we would give up and go off, leaving him to rot wherever he was. Sooner or later he would show up, all mad because we didn't keep looking for him. And we would all get mad because he wasn't playing the game the way it is supposed to be played.[3]

It is no fun if no finding is involved, he goes on to say as he stares out of his window at a kid hidden so well the others cannot find him. Finally, Fulghum yells out at him, "Get found, Kid!"

That's the way it is with us and God, except that we are hidden so well and only halfway want to be found. Even when we want to be found, we don't know how, and we miss it often when it happens. It's not that we are so well hidden that God can't find us. Rather, we have predetermined what being found is like. We demand to be found on our own terms, while God often quietly sits in our hiding place waiting for us to acknowledge that we have been found. Finding often means acknowledging that God has been beside us all along. Or, we may be so comfortable in our hiding places that we convince ourselves we can't be found. The cost of playing the game this way is to never experience the friendship of God in a personal way.

Many of us are hidden really well. We've learned to keep quiet when God is near. When we do come out of hiding, it is always when we want to and not as part of the game of faith. We spend years, or even lifetimes, playing hide-and-seek by ourselves, never experiencing the God who is "It."

Notes

[1]Frederick Buechner, *Wishful Thinking* (San Francisco: Harper & Row, 1973) 32

[2]Ibid., *The Final Beast* (San Francisco: Harper & Row, 1965) 175.

[3]Robert Fulghum, *All I Really Needed to Know I Learned in Kindergarten* (New York: Ivy Books, 1988) 54.

Chapter 3

Looking for God
at Church

It was known as the "Exit to Ministry" class, taught by a retired pastor whose lectures were filled mostly with references to all the people he knew. A required class all seminarians had to take, there was no chance of obtaining the diploma we had paid all of that money to get without sitting through two hours a week of name-dropping. The last week of class was a light at the end of the tunnel, however, and most students arrived with a renewed sense of vigor, knowing that in a matter of days they would become professional Christians.

Michael was one of these students, although he did not share the emerging enthusiasm of his classmates. Those who knew him were aware he had divorced his wife several months earlier, and many churches are not interested in hiring damaged goods. He was a good student who excelled in his classes. Ironically, he had made an A in a marriage enrichment class at the same time his divorce became final. All the work to excel had left him doubting whatever sense of calling had brought him to the seminary in the first place. He never spoke in the Exit to Ministry class, preferring to remain detached and observe the future leaders of the church as they described everything they planned to accomplish.

On the last day of this last class, the professor asked if anyone had any final words before graduation. Several students immediately stated they hoped to be as successful in the kingdom of God as the professor had been, which probably meant one day they would drop as many names as he had. After a few of these testimonials, Michael raised his hand. Silence greeted his first and only participation in the course. The professor smiled and invited him to say whatever he had on his mind. Waiting a few moments to ensure he had everyone's attention, he cleared his throat and smiled.

"I think we have all made a big mistake," he began. He had their complete attention. "We're all sitting here dreaming about becoming big-time ministers in very wealthy churches with big crowds of people paying us large salaries. Every one of us is talking about preaching being the most important thing we will ever do, and what we are really saying is how good it feels to stand in the pulpit and feel like we are the center of the universe for twenty minutes each Sunday morning. I don't think this is what it is all about. If Jesus were to come back right now, I believe the first thing he would do is rent a bulldozer and level almost every damn one of them."

Attention quickly turned into anarchy. People began yelling at Michael. The professor was talking loudly in some vain attempt to regain control of the class, but an honest opinion had been spoken; and any kind of truth, once let out of the bag, is so painful that people's reactions are drastic. Michael simply collected his things and left the room. He then enrolled in another school and became a lawyer. Everyone else went on to follow in the footsteps of the professor who, thankfully, went into a real retirement soon afterwards far away from the classroom.

Those whose livelihoods are not reliant upon the church may be quicker to appreciate Michael's opinion. Is what we have really what God intended? Can churches preoccupied with buildings, budgets, religious entertainment, and services built around the sermon also accommodate the needs of real people with profound needs? If people go to church looking for God, why do they end up finding all kinds of religious things but no divine encounters? Are ministers much more than professional Christians, paid to do what they ask others to do for free?

This song by minstrel Jimmy Buffett captures the feelings many people have for church these days:

> Where's the church?
> Who took the steeple?
> Religions in the hands of crazy ass people.

> Television preachers with bad hair and dimples,
> the God's honest trust is
> it's not that simple.
> It's the Christian in you,
> it's the pagan in me;
> It's the Muslim in him,
> she's Catholic ain't she?
> It's that born-again look,
> it's the WASP and the Jew.
> Tell me what's going on!
> I ain't got a clue![1]

No doubt the church we get is not necessarily the one we want. Our expectation is usually more than what the church can possibly deliver on. Why, then, do we continue to profess allegiance to a church that does not live up to our wishes, or after we have given up anyway and only attend when we feel required? Most of us seem to really want a church that actually does deliver God. Yet, too many of us settle for something far less.

While the church has not been particularly useful in facilitating encounters with God, it has been very successful in delivering some things.

Things the Church Offers to Those Looking for God

- sermons, usually about God, but always with the possibility they can end up being about something else
- religious music
- dried-out food at Wednesday night suppers
- committees (some even have a committee on committees)
- appeals for money
- covered dish suppers or the opportunity to feed Kentucky Fried Chicken to a lot of people
- an occasion to dress up
- choirs that are increasingly accompanied by taped music
- chances to take exotic, or at least across-town, trips at a group discount with people you wouldn't normally go anywhere with

• some safety-in-numbers security in knowing that the other people
who attend are at about the same place you are when looking for
God

The church has proven itself to be quite effective in offering
these and other activities for those choosing to attend. Many
churches now include specialized services especially designed for
young people (kind of a training for adult church); coffee and
doughnuts during Sunday School; and even bowling alleys, basket-
ball courts, softball teams, and racketball courts. Unfortunately,
most of us do not need church to get our fill of such things.

The church offers a great many things that may challenge, frus-
trate, encourage, disappoint, or be exceptionally beautiful; but it
rarely gives us what we really want: God. It's funny. This wanting of
God almost always begins away from the church. Finding God
always starts with ourselves, usually by ourselves. Something
happens, according to John Shea.

A friend dies; a child smiles us into wonder; an old lady refuses
to be old; an adolescent finds a way out; a secret weakness is
exposed; we are unexpectedly kissed.
First something happens.
A short fall is suddenly without bottom; an expectation is
reversed; a comforting self-image is shaken.
First something happens.
At the center of our best effort we discover our worst mo-
tive. Our perfect ploy fails, and their sloppiest plan succeeds.
In single-minded pursuit of one goal, we blithely achieve the
opposite. When all retreat at the sight of the dead, we stay and
stare and do not know why. First something happens.
In these moments, and many more, we are thrown back on
ourselves. More precisely, we are thrown back into the Mystery we share with one another. These moments trigger an
awareness of the More, a Presence, an Encompassing, a Whole
within which we come and go. This awareness is an inescap-
able relatedness to Mystery and does not wait for a polite
introduction. It bursts unbidden upon our ordinary routine,
demands total attention, and insists we dialogue. At these times
we may scream or laugh or dance or cry or fall silent. But

whatever our response, it is raw prayer, the returning of human
impulse to the touch of God.[2]

The something that happens catapults us into an awareness normally not present, but one we desperately want to explore. More
often than not, it is some everyday event that is part of living a normal life. A friend dies. Something unexpectedly goes right—or
wrong. Someone says something, and the reaction is as though the
blinds open to expose a nighttime sky. It is so dark we can't really
see anything, but we look anyway, focusing intently on shapes both
imagined and, if we are lucky, real.

At this point, all our capacities are at their fullest. We see
clearer. We hear everything. Our imagination runs wild. Terrifying
and exiciting thoughts are born. Our desire for God is intense. We
want to create. We want to share. We are content. It was at such a
point that Moses took off his shoes and talked to God, Paul fell to
his face on the Damascus Road, John saw his revelation, and Elijah
heard the small voice. It is at such a point that we are aware of the
possibilities of God. We are content enough when experiencing it,
but, after it passes, we are left wanting more.

How do we pursue such a feeling? It is not a tangible or con-
tainable feeling but a series of fleeting images. Many of us quickly
put it all behind us and go ahead with our lives. For those who
struggle with the feeling, however, two important realizations
occur. First, we comprehend how small and insignificant we are
within the universe. We may express the admission in different
ways—we are powerless over drugs or alcohol, our marriage is in
trouble, the children are not coming back, or we deserved what we
got—but each says the same thing: "I am not in control." This
quickly leads to the second admission: "I need help." Once we
comprehend the fact that we cannot succeed alone, we are open to
the possibility of God in our lives.

In and of themselves, these are profound confessions, and inter-
estingly, church is merely one of the many places they are realized.
In most cases, the discovery comes somewhere other than church. It
could be over a cup of coffee at home late at night or in a crowded
bar over a beer.

After such moments, the need for affirmation from others becomes important to us. We seek out friends in order to share what we have experienced. Our spouse hears a lengthy dissertation on what we are going through. We want to hear if others have lived through the same thing. We go to church hoping against hope that the possibility of God becomes an actual encounter with God. (Whistling in the dark is how Frederick Buechner describes it.) At this point the church most often lets us down by seemingly focusing on everything except what interests us most.

When we show up with a determination to earnestly explore what led to our self-confessions, the church offers us a vast menu of details we do not necessarily want.

Things the Church Insists on Offering

- theological words you can't pronounce
- doctrine or a pre-packaged set of beliefs about things that don't have much to do with what you're feeling at the moment
- music that is too depressing or too happy for the mood you're in
- church history (if I had wanted it, I would have taken the course)
- distractions from the feelings that brought you to the church in the first place or when someone tries to get you to do something you really don't want to
- foreign languages you don't understand
- any kind of clutter in front of the task at hand such as filling out pledge cards, being asked to join the choir, or an invitation to become a member of the church
- political speeches
- advice to hang in there and you'll be able to work it out
- people who turn their backs on you (including the priest or minister)

Each of these may or may not become important, but at the time they are utterly insignificant to what we are looking for. What we want is God. What we too often get is other stuff in the name of God. We want to get to the bottom of those feelings that brought about our self-confessions, but it seems as though all we are offered are more things to do. We want to explore the unchartered territory of our lives, but we get an order of worship. We want to know that we are part of a larger whole, but we get our name on the church rolls. We want personal encounters, but we get a letter from the minister. No wonder so many of us give up on church (although our names stay on the roll forever) and take our search for God elsewhere. As someone put it, churches would rather count sheep than feed them.

Ironically, we know precisely what we want when we go to church. Recognizing that the feelings we have experienced are deep and profound, we do not expect someone to tell us what it is all about. Nor do we expect a minister to personally introduce us to God (although this would be nice). The things we want are much simpler.

Things We Want from the Church

- an understanding of what we have been through
- sympathy because we have admitted we are out of control and in need of help
- encouragement from others that we are at the right place with the right questions
- more exposure to the sense of mystery and wonder that motivated us in the first place
- help in obtaining a better focus on the mystery of God
- a sense of wonder
- the chance to be tangibly accepted just as we are
- help in changing so that we begin the process of becoming what we feel God wants us to be
- relationships with others who we believe are useful to our purpose of finding God
- to experience the sense of mystery and wonder again

What we want is so simple, but what we get takes several full-time and part-time staff people to prepare. Through the years, the church has institutionalized human relationships and interaction so much that the words no longer carry a real meaning. We call one another brother and sister and may as well be saying nothing at all. Yet the longing for what the words mean is very real to us, and so we attend church where they say all the right things but actually do very little. People come to church needing to be touched, but are instructed to focus outward to a God they only hear about.

Other expressions of brotherhood and sisterhood have emerged in recent years and now challenge the church. Community building workshops take place across the country, providing a viable way for people to actualize the things they begin searching for in a church. Support groups of every type imaginable continue to grow and keep the focus on the participants without cluttering the agenda with buildings, budgets, orders of worship, or maintenance of stained glass windows.

The church (Protestant and Catholic) places primary emphasis on salvation of the individual. Come to the church and be saved. Most of us go through the motions because we are still motivated by the desire to experience the mystery and wonder that led to our self-confessions. After salvation then, what happens? As Robert Moore and Douglas Gillette wrote, "Often very little. Frequently churches are not set up with the vision to provide anything more."[3] Because of this, many people feel church is obsolete.

Too many churches run the risk of trying to convince people that the goods they are selling are the ones people really want. Unfortunately, most of the time they are not. People are smart enough to figure out other ways to look for God, and God is certainly capable of attending Alcoholics Anonymous meetings or a community building workshop.

Some will protest, of course, that the church is the only true way to look for God. No doubt they will cite Scripture that the gates of hell shall not prevail against it. There is certainly no doubt as to what Scripture states, but my classmate Michael's opinion leads one to a very relevant question: Is the church we have the one God intended? There are legitimate justifications to think it is not.

Jesus never seemed to be very interested in the institutional matters that are part of the modern church. At no time did Jesus ever build a building, establish an operating budget, form a committee, or write any policies and procedures for how people should follow God. Rather, he spent a lot of time talking with people, helping them meet their needs, and demonstrating what it means to follow God. Too many churches have forgotten the art of personal interaction. As a result, the church itself needs saving. For this to happen, the church must regain the art of community.

It is probably not coincidental that many other expressions of community have developed in recent years. A number of them, such as those listed above, are not overtly religious but seem to meet the needs of people looking for God and community. Other expressions of community were found in the church, however, and met the needs of a people looking for God.

Several years ago, many third world countries were having difficulty finding enough priests to conduct Mass. Individuals began to compensate by developing their own ways of worship without the constraints of institutional religion. Ernest Cardinal recorded the conversations of normal people in Solentiname, Nicaragua, as they discussed the Bible and their own longings for God, publishing them as *The Gospel in Solentiname.* The process by which the commentaries were "spoken," and then written, is likely more in tune with what people actually want when they go looking for God in a church. Cardinal described the process:

> Many of these commentaries were made in the church, at Sunday Mass. Others were made in a thatched hut opposite the church, used for meetings and the communal lunch after Mass. Occasionally, we would have Mass and the Gospel dialogue in the open air on other islands, or in a small house that we could get to by rowing along a beautiful river through very tropical vegetation.
>
> Each Sunday we first would distribute copies of the Gospels to those who could read. There were some who couldn't, especially among the elderly and those who lived on islands far away from school. One of those who could read the best (generally a boy or a girl) would read aloud the entire passage on which we were going to comment. Then we discussed it verse by verse.[4]

The final product was a series of commentaries not burdened by theology or doctrine and a people who grasped a clear understanding of God through the reading of the Bible. There was no order of worship, no budget restrictions, no building concerns, nor any real leadership. Collectively, people gathered and simply shared what they thought. Such an approach is probably closer to what Jesus had in mind when he collected groups of people and told stories.

There is no need to worry about the future of the church. It will be around forever. It is harder for a church to die than just about anything else. After all, institutions exist to perpetuate themselves, and the modern church is an institution. Given a choice between following God into an unknown country or making prudent decisions to secure itself for the future, the church will almost always choose the latter.

The good news is this: God is not confined to the four walls of a religious building. God is much bigger. A game of hide-and-seek is forever taking place where God pops into our lives to remind us that we don't necessarily need church to have an interaction. While church continues to demand that we come inside, God is inviting us to come out and play.

Notes

[1]Jimmy Buffett, "Fruitcakes" (Margaritaville Records, MCA, Coral Reefer Music, BMI/Publick Ptmoaine Music BMI, 1994).

[2]John Shea, *The Hour of the Unexpected* (Niles IL: Argus Communications, 1977) 9.

[3]Robert Moore and Douglas Gillette, *The Kingdom Within* (New York: Avon Books, 1992) 242.

[4]Ernesto Cardinal, *The Gospel in Solentiname* (New York: Orbis Books, 1984) vii-viii.

Chapter 4

Looking for God in
"Leaders of the Lost"

Most ministers and other zealots are forever saying we are lost. Instead of telling us what we really want to hear—that God will find us—they have the gall to tell *us* to find God. If we knew how to find God, then we wouldn't be lost. Why is it so hard for most clergy to get this through their heads? Most everyone would like to be given the choice between remaining lost and being found. They would immediately say, "Here I am!" But most ministers don't say a great deal about the finding part. They merely remind us of what we already know.

"Come be lost with us in church" seems to be the real message, and the congregation is no longer a game of hide-and-seek, but Sardines instead. This is not all bad, says Robert Fulghum.

> In Sardines the person who is "It" goes and hides, and everybody goes looking for him. When you find him, you get in with him and hide there with him. Pretty soon everybody is hiding together, all stacked in a small space like puppies in a pile. And pretty soon somebody giggles, and somebody laughs, and everybody gets found. Medieval theologians even described God in hide-and-seek terms, calling him *Deus Absconditus.* But me, I think old God is a Sardine player and will be found the same way everybody gets found in Sardines—by the sound of laughter of those heaped together at the end.[1]

It is frustrating when ministers go on forever reminding us we are lost and encouraging us to find God rather than be found. (It seems as though the clergy cannot even remember what game is being played.) When we ask how, the kindly response is usually something to the effect of "Just pray and invite him to come into your heart." So we pray and invite God into our hearts. Typically, ministers are very upbeat after this occurs and act as though the entire matter has been resolved. As far as they are concerned, we are no longer lost. Of course, they immediately launch into a diatribe of how we now need a church home and what we need to do in order to join.

Soon enough, with all the things required of us, we completely forget why we originally talked to a minister. We are too busy to know we are lost. Until something happens—a crisis occurs, a friend dies, something wells up inside asking if this is all there is—we are right back where we began. Sooner or later, we remember we are lost, or at least we can't find God, and the search starts all over again.

Why are ministers so convincing when it comes to seemingly finding God? Part of it is likely our own desire to be convinced. Ministers tell us the answer is as simple as a prayerful invitation and opening of our hearts to God. Because we do not want to appear stupid, we follow the instructions, open our eyes, and claim that certainly we have found God—although we are not quite certain what we have found. Ministers are such consummate sales-persons that only later—after we have joined the church, given away a great deal of time and money, and still are left wanting in a time of need—do we realize we have purchased damaged goods, or at least the goods we have bought have not prevented us from again being damaged.

Bruce, a homeless alcoholic and friend of mine, was at least honest enough to respond to a certain minister's simple instructions by growing angry and asking: "Pray? Hell, I've been praying for weeks! I've invited God into my heart a thousand times, and I still don't know what that means. My heart is nothing more than a mus-cle that pumps blood to my brain and my toes. How is God supposed to get in there?" He then left the office claiming he stood a better chance of finding God without clerical help.

We have high expectations of the clergy, and they are consis-tently not met. When we want something or someone but cannot articulate what it is, ministers are quite busy selling what it must be.

Clergy are a strange breed. Utterly convinced they know how God wants things, they project an image of perfection. This is likely based upon the biblical mandate to be perfect as God in heaven is perfect. So ministers work at being perfect as some way of setting an example for the rest of us. Consequently, many of them have learned to do some things remarkably well.

For example, most male ministers can keep their socks up all the time. In heaven, I suppose everyone's socks always stay up all the time—and ministers want us to be able to see a little glimpse of heaven on earth. This is evidently such an important point that some seminary professors have been known to stress the magnitude of keeping the socks up at all times as part of one's witness. (I am not making this up!)

Combing their hair is something else most ministers accomplish with exceptional aptitude. Female clergy either like the limp, stringy, simple look of an artist too concerned with things other than appearance; or they go to the opposite extreme by opting for really big, powerful-looking hair in some attempt to make themselves more grand than they really are. Most male ministers appear to have their hair cut at Dairy Queen with a swirling mass on top of normally bald heads. Some kind of concrete is then poured on top so the hair cannot be blown out of place even in a hurricane. Many people are convinced that ministers take their hair off before they go to sleep, placing it on a little stand next to the bed.

Ministers dress better than most people—also part of the clerical image. In days gone by, you could always count on the clergy to wear basic black—either a robe or some Puritan suit—and there was always some reassurance in being able to pick the ministers out in a crowd. It is not so simple now. Many ministers are under the impression they are employed by a Fortune 500 company and dress accordingly. Taken collectively, the clergy seems to send this primary message: "Image is everything." Several things appear to be consistent in the way they present themselves.

Things Ministers Want Us to Believe

- Ministers know where God is all the time.
- God always tells the clergy in advance.
- Ministers always speak for God.
- Ministers never sin, or at least it was a very long time ago (in which case they tell the story again and again).
- It is more fun to go somewhere with your minister than with most anyone else.
- Everything ministers say is important.
- Ministers read a lot of books. (Some do; most don't.)
- Ministers have perfect marriages.
- Ministers really are poor. (The Cadillac out front was a gift!)
- If you attend church long enough, you'll find God.

The fact of the matter is ministers are no different from anyone else. They simply have the luxury of working a job that allows them to think about God all the time. Because they have just as hard a time as the rest of us finding God, many grow frustrated and begin focusing on other things. You can hardly blame them. Wanting to be as successful as anyone else, clergy recognize that finding God doesn't happen very often, and, even when it does, God doesn't hang around too long. So they conceive other ways to project an image of success. Buildings, for example, are one way ministers proclaim their success. The bigger the church building, the better the minister. So building campaigns are conducted, and the church becomes a campus. Unfortunately, the people who attend are still asking the same question: How can I find God?

Ministers don't know, so they come up with other activities to keep their congregations busy. They organize trips for the senior citizens, plan bingo nights, get involved in politics, or increase their staffs because they're too busy thinking up all these things to do. As Lewis Grizzard wrote,

> It's not easy being a preacher these days. Preachers have to work harder than ever before keeping their flocks in line what with temptations at a new all-time high. I suppose the really big-time preachers, like Billy Graham and Oral Roberts and

Jerry Falwell, have it made, though. Every time I pick up the newspaper there's a story about one of those heavyweight television preachers making a trip to Russia, or speaking out on international issues, or having a vision that tells him to go out and raise a few million bucks. I always wonder when those guys find time to work on their sermons. When do they visit the sick and marry people and preach funerals?[2]

All of this preoccupation with image is a telling point for the clergy. They are earning their keep by projecting the best facsimile of God they can. After all, ministers are nothing more than professional Christians, persons who get paid to do what they ask you to do for free. Other than this, ministers are no different from anyone else. Frederick Buechner got to the root of it in his book *Wishful Thinking.*

The first ministers were the twelve disciples. There is no evidence that Jesus chose them because they were brighter or nicer than other people. In fact the New Testament record suggests that they were continually missing the point, jockeying for position, and, when the chips were down, interested in nothing so much as saving their own skins. Their sole qualification seems to have been their initial willingness to rise to their feet when Jesus said, "Follow me."[3]

Part of the problem could be that many ministers are not following God as much as they are pursuing other things. It is likely that more mothers have called their sons and daughters into the ministry than God. Confused about what got them into the business in the first place, too many clergy go to great pains to point out how different and unique they are. They erect barriers against other people who are searching for the same God as they are. Trying so hard to be pastors, they forget how to act as partners. Wanting to be leaders, too many ministers lose the art of following God's lead. In the end, most ministers are leaders of the lost, overseeing an institutional mass of people wandering around a spiritual desert much like the children of Israel.

The sense of expectation ministers have is much higher than what we actually want from them. While they are focusing on producing great things for God, we want something much simpler.

Things We Want in a Minister

- We want a minister to have a decent conversation with, filled with honest exclamations such as "I don't know" and "It's o.k."
- We want a minister who offers an assurance that, regardless of what we say, it is received in loving understanding.
- We want a minister who will listen more than talk and who will say something worth hearing when he or she does speak.
- We want a minister who will grieve with us and be smart enough to say when it is time to get on with our lives.
- We want a minister who will lead the celebration of weddings, conduct funerals, and remind us about playing hide-and-seek with God should we forget.

That is all we really want. Of course, we get a ton of other things we never asked for. What we want from our minister is a friend; what we get is a religious leader. We desire someone with whom we can express ourselves, but we end up with someone trying to prove himself or herself. No wonder the state of religion is so screwed-up! Our clergy have no idea where they are leading us.

Clarence Jordan, who looked for God with people of different races in a Christian community, once said that if you want to follow God, find out where the rest of the world is heading, and go in the opposite direction. It seems too many ministers are leading their congregations in the exact same direction as the McDonald's corporation with an emphasis on bite-size theology, Ronald McDonald entertainment, and moving up the ladder of orthodoxy. It makes sense. Churches are institutions that employ clergy who perpetuate the organization. There's little room in the church for ministers determined to go to any lengths in leading their congregations in a search for God. Clarence Jordan told a story of such a minister.

During the days of segregation in the South, he was invited to speak at a Southern Baptist church in North Carolina. After looking the place up on a map, he reasoned it must be some swank, aristocratic, liberal church wanting someone to pat them on the back for their broad-minded views on race. What he found instead was a little mill-town church on the edge of the city that had grown up and engulfed it. Built to seat 300, there were twice that many people present for the service. The amazing thing was the people were white and black all mixed together. The choir was mixed. After the service was over, the minister announced there would be dinner on the grounds, and everyone went in the front yard, where the entire city could see them, and ate. "In those days," Clarence noted, "it was one thing for black and white folks to worship together; it's another thing for them to eat together."

He asked the minister, "You know, this is a rather amazing thing to me. Were you integrated before the Supreme Court decision?"

"What decision?" the minister replied.

The motivation was the church's collective search for God. The minister explained how it happened. "Well, back during the Depression, I was a worker here in this little mill. I didn't have any education. I couldn't even read and write. I got somebody to read the Bible to me, and I was moved to give my heart to the Lord, and later, I felt the call of the Lord to preach."

"This little church here was too poor to have a preacher, and I just volunteered. They accepted me, and I started preaching. Someone read to me in there where God is no respecter of persons, and I preached that."

Clarence asked how that was received by the church.

"Well," the minister replied, "the deacons came around to me after that sermon and said, 'Now, brother pastor, we not only don't let a nigger spend the night in this town; we don't even let him pass through. Now, we don't want that kind of preaching you're giving us.' "

Clarence asked, "What did you do?"

"Well," he said, "I fired them deacons."

"How come they didn't fire you?"

"Well," the minister replied, "they never had hired me. I just volunteered."

"Did you have any more trouble with them?"

"Yeah. They came back at me again."

"What did you do with them that time?" Clarence asked.

"I turned them out. I told them that anybody who didn't know any more about the gospel of Jesus than that not only shouldn't be an officer in the church, he shouldn't be a member of it. I had to put them out."

"Did you have to put anybody else out?"

"Well, I preached awfully hard, and I finally preached them down to two." "But," the minister said, "those two were committed. I made sure that any time after that, anybody who came into my church understood that they were giving their life to Jesus Christ, and they were going to have to be serious about it. What you see here is a result of that."[4]

Here is an example of a minister who concentrated on leading his lost congregation in their search for God by using the Bible as an instruction of how people are supposed to live with one another when playing hide-and-seek with God. He pretended to be nothing other than who he was: a simple, former mill worker who listened to what the Bible said and tried to implement it in his life. He refused to shy away from some of the more difficult passages in the Bible and would take the search anywhere it took him. In this case, the search meant exploring community among the races in the segregated South. History proves that few ministers were willing to look for God during that time.

Such an approach is certainly contrary to the approach of most clergy. Many ministers seem more concerned with job security than with playing hide-and-seek with God. As a result, they become little more than leaders of the lost. Instead of searching for God, they try to fill their congregation's void by being God, or at least being what they believe God would be. No wonder so many churches are simply places where people get together from time to time in God's name.

No wonder so many of us are frustrated with the clergy. They prostitute their mission to the world by reducing it to keeping pace with the population growth of the community. They externalize their mission so it becomes wrapped up in statistics and structures.

They set for themselves numerical goals that become a substitute for any reconciling thrust into the world. They become status seekers who call upon the rest of us to assist them in finding it.[5]

Yet, in spite of this frustration, we long for good religious leaders. Even those who have nothing to do with church, rarely attending, are on the lookout for a minister from time to time. We want someone to perform the wedding, conduct the funeral, or simply discuss things we do not understand. The fields are ripe for harvest for those willing to be ministers-at-large, volunteering to offer their services to a congregation that does not formally exist.

This is a place where my own search for God has carried me. Because I am an ordained minister but do not represent a church, I receive a great many inquiries from people who do not consider themselves to be religious. Some are comical.

One night, after arriving home late, I was rummaging around the kitchen looking for something to eat when the telephone rang. The caller introduced himself as the owner of a local restaurant and asked if I was a minister. I assured him I was. "Do you marry people?" he asked. "Yes," I responded. He said, "We have a couple at the restaurant who would like to get married. Could you perform the ceremony?" "When?" I asked. "Now," he said. I told him I did not perform weddings on demand. Before I could explain why, he asked if I could recommend someone else. I did, and he hung up.

Most of the time when people want me to be their minister, it is more serious in nature. A couple of friends have decided to get married and asks how they should best prepare for their new lives together. A child gets in trouble, and the parent wants to talk about it. A son is tragically killed, and I am asked to stop by the house and visit the family. A wife is hospitalized, and her husband wants me to pray for her recovery. A young man loses his job and just wants someone to talk with. A girl becomes pregnant and asks me to help her tell her parents. These real-life and paramount issues in people's lives are the motivation to seek God or, failing to find God, look for a minister who will respond to the immediate need.

It is not the institutional agenda of the church we want so much as it is a personable minister. We don't want a pastor as much as a compassionate friend. Many clergy freely do these things for anyone who asks. Others are so caught up in the policies and procedures of the church, however, they fail to minister when asked. People want a minister strong enough to be lost with them, not someone else simply denying they are as lost as everyone else.

Notes

[1]Robert Fulghum, *All I Really Needed to Know I Learned in Kindergarten* (New York: Ivy Books, 1988) 56.

[2]Lewis Grizzard, "Good Men of God," *A Collection of Classic Southern Humor*, ed. George William Koon (Atlanta: Peachtree Publisher, 1984) 154.

[3]Frederick Buechner, *Wishful Thinking* (San Francisco: Harper & Row, 1973) 62.

[4]Clarence Jordan, *The Substance of Faith* (New York: Association Press, 1972) 43-44.

[5]Robert Raines, *New Life in the Church* (San Francisco: Harper & Row, 1980) 4.

Chapter 5

Looking for God in Poor People

A great many people on the edges of the church claim that God is easily found in working with the poor. Of course, this is shocking because, while we sometimes hear our ministers say that God loves the poor, we rarely hear that God likes to hang around poor people. Besides, many are not accustomed to visiting churches that have a lot of poor people also attending. It stands to reason that if God is easily found with the poor, then ministers would be getting more to attend. This is obviously not the case, so we immediately doubt if God is any more with the poor than in the churches we attend. Yet, a number of people say that in order to find God, we must get involved with the poor.

No doubt the Bible spends a lot of time talking about the poor. Jesus talked about "good news to the poor" and being judged by how we respond to the hungry, the poor, the naked, the imprisoned, the sick, and the stranger. There are all of those verses about giving away what we have, inviting the homeless into our own homes, and going the extra mile for someone who needs a ride. Saint James even went so far as to say,

> Listen, my beloved brothers and sisters. Has not God chosen the poor in the world to be rich in faith and to be heirs of the kingdom that he has promised to those who love him? (2:5).

Jim Wallis of the Sojourners Community wrote:

> In the Old Testament, the subject of the poor is the second most prominent theme. Idolatry is the first, and the two are often connected. In the New Testament, one out of every sixteen verses is about the poor![1]

According to some people's interpretation of the Bible, to know God is to get involved with the poor.

Such religious explanations confuse many of us. What does getting involved with poor people have to do with finding God? Does this mean that rich people are called upon to find God by getting involved with the poor? Are we supposed to give up everything we have or just some things? How long are we to assume that we must involve ourselves with the poor? How come we never deal with these biblical passages in Sunday School?

The fact of the matter is, we really don't want to get too involved with poor people as a way of finding God. We would much rather look for God in other ways. It would be one thing to spend a little bit of time with the poor, but no one wants to get carried away. To many folks, a personal relationship with God is a private matter only to be discussed with our closest friends or in church. Besides, most of us feel we are poor, or at least just getting by, ourselves. Poverty is always a relative concept, and, while most of us recognize we are not as poor as the starving masses we see broadcast on our television screens, we also know we have bills to pay and are not as rich as the people we read about in the newspapers.

Although most of us don't take the time to list them, there are many reasons why we don't want to get too involved with poor people.

Reasons Why We Don't Want to Look for God in the Poor

• Poor people are different from us, and we would feel uncomfortable being with them for too long—and God doesn't want us to be uncomfortable.
• God is everywhere, not just with poor people; and if God is everywhere, then we don't need to go looking anywhere.
• Religion is a private matter between God and me, and poor people don't need to be involved in my religion.
• Poor people don't come to church, and I don't want to waste my time with people who don't come to church.
• People who are poor will obtain great riches in heaven, but I have to use mine now.

- My minister doesn't seem to think it is important that I get involved with poor people.
- The Sunday School only mentions the issue occasionally.
- God must want some people to be poor because that is the way things are.
- God is calling me to deal with other things, and I must remain focused on them right now.
- Poverty is not a religious issue; the Bible meant "poor in spirit," which could be anyone—not just poor people.

Dealing with poverty is a complex enough social problem, so many people feel it should not also be considered a spiritual one. Our spiritual lives are complex enough without the frustrations of involving ourselves with poor people. Spiritual searches demand a tremendous amount of focus and energy, while poor people will suck most of our resources out of us if we let them. The demands of the poor are even greater than those made by our religions!

Yet, each of the major religions places a great deal of emphasis on how people respond to the poor. Why is this importance attached to one's search for God? It would be so much easier if we could focus all our attention on loving God. We have a hard-enough time doing that! No doubt most of us focus on our individual searches for God. The great religious institutions of today have reduced one's relationship with God to a private matter. As Os Guinness said,

> Where religion still survives in the modern world, no matter how passionate or "committed" the individual believer may be, it amounts to little more than a private preference, a spare-time hobby, a leisure pursuit.[2]

God's emphasis on the poor is one way of preventing us from reducing our spiritual development to matters of a private nature.

Joe is a senior vice-president of a bank in charge of the trust department. His job is to take other people's money, invest it for them, and make a profit for both the customer and the bank. He is very good at what he does, having held the position for quite some time. On the other hand, Joe is also a very spiritual person. He reads a great many religious books, attends church faithfully, and volunteers his time with various community efforts. One of these volunteer efforts was serving as a member of the board of directors of a homeless shelter. Because of this role, he agreed to attend a worship service at the shelter one evening.

Joe arrived on time and took his seat amid the homeless men and women who had gathered to worship. The leaders for the night's service were from the Bearean Bible Chapel, a nearby congregation that had expressed concern for the homeless since the shelter had first opened.

The worship was a celebration of the fact that people had been able to survive. They gave thanks to God for being able to live through another day, for being able to eat and sleep in the shelter that night, and for all the bountiful blessings the Lord continued to bestow upon them. They sang songs, clapped their hands, and spent a lot of time hugging in fellowship. When each of the participants was given the opportunity to testify, Joe was struck that so many homeless people offered thanks and praise to God for all they had received. He knew that many had nothing but the clothes on their backs and a few coins in their pockets, yet they still praised God. He thought of everything he owned—the house outside the city, his friends, and the money tucked away in the bank. A lump rose in his throat as he joined in the fellowship and became an active worshiper with the ragtag congregation.[3]

There is no question that work with the poor generates one of two reactions in people. Either we are repulsed by them, or we are enlightened as a result of our efforts. There rarely seems to be much middle ground. It is much the same when believing in God or exploring our spiritual lives. Either we do not like what a spiritual search means for us, or we recognize the positive results of such a journey. It is all or nothing.

Perhaps the poor are here for a special reason that is directly related to our searches for God. The poor remind us there are other people whose needs are always more than our own. They force us to recognize that no matter how difficult things are in our own lives, someone else has it worse. The poor have a way of throwing in our faces that they are forced to rely solely on God, while we have God plus a great many other things. We have a place to live, friends, a family who cares, enough money to buy food. We have God—plus!

The poor merely have God. The Scriptures are forever challenging us to express our love of God by caring for the poor. Gustavo Gutierrez affirmed this challenge in his book *The Power of the Poor in History:*

> We stand before a God who is a challenge, a God who over-
> turns our human categories, a God who will not be reduced to
> our mode of thinking, and who judges us on the basis of our
> concrete, historical actions toward the poor. . . . Now we face a
> God who cuts straight through the love of a liar—the love that
> forgets sisters and brothers and pretends to direct itself toward
> God instead, pretends to direct itself "spiritually" (more to
> domesticate God than to feel itself called to into question by
> [God] . . . in order to know and love God one must come to
> grips with the concrete life situation of the poor today, and
> undertake the radical transformation of a society that makes
> them poor.[4]

If this is true, then God is changing the rules of the spiritual game of hide-and-seek by forcing us to play with people we would rather not associate with and look in places we would just as soon not go. This is contrary to believing that religion is a private matter between us and God. Including the poor in our spiritual searches only complicates the matter of finding God. The more people involved, the more likely we are to be confused about our religion. Why would the Scriptures continue to emphasize the poor when all we want is simple instruction on how to establish a personal relationship with God? Why would God want us to do something as difficult as getting involved with the poor when all we want is to understand God? Why does God want us to do something that would make us so uncomfortable when we are searching for peace in our lives?

Reasons Why God Wants Us to Play with Poor People

• God wants to remind all of us that we are God's children and are to act like one big happy family that should have more to do with one another.

- Like most parents, God gives the most attention to the children experiencing the most problems while asking the other brothers and sisters to help out.
- Like most children, when God focuses extra attention on a brother or a sister, we act up, often by throwing a spiritual temper tantrum, in an attempt to get the spotlight back on us.
- God wants to remind us that no matter how much help we need, someone else always needs more.
- God wants to remind us that no matter how little we have, someone else always has less; therefore, we should be thankful for what we have.
- God wants to remind us that we all have the ability to make a significant difference in someone else's life.
- God wants us to know that being involved with the poor makes us quit thinking so much about ourselves—and God wants us to think less about ourselves.
- God wants us to think about new things, and poor people force us to think about things we would usually never consider.
- God wants us to try new things, and poor people force us to do things we would usually never consider.
- Being involved with poor people forces us to rely on God when looking for a solution to problems too overwhelming to solve on our own.

Thinking of things in this way makes a lot of sense. Most parents want their children to be part of a happy family, helping out when a brother or sister is experiencing problems and being mature enough not to throw a temper tantrum when they're not the center of the show. Mothers want their sons to learn to be thankful for what they have and mindful that so many others have less. Fathers want their daughters to make a positive difference in the world, to be bold enough to try new things, and not to be afraid of change. Parents want their children to know they can be relied on when the chips are down and life seems too big to face alone.

We like to think of God as a father or a mother. We also like to think of ourselves as God's children. Doesn't it make sense then that God would want us to learn the same lessons any parent desires to teach their children? Viewing the poor as God's way of teaching us these lessons make a great deal of sense. Of course, most of us prefer to think of ourselves as only children. This leads to our preoccupation with our personal, and private, relationships with God. By acting as though we are the only thing that matters, and our own spiritual searches demand most of our attention, we forget we are simply part of the family of God.

God so strongly identifies with the poor, often becoming a poor person in the hide-and-seek game of faith, we are given a tangible way of seeing things that are holy and full of spiritual meaning. The poor are also God's way of saying that we are not alone in our spiritual quests. Like many journeys into the woods of doubt, we will often receive help and guidance from the most unexpected sources, while admitting that the people and things we thought would be most useful in our pilgrimages are not. God claims divine presence on the earth and in our midst through the poor. Just as many people refuse to accept a God who will walk among us, many will not embrace poor people as a way of communicating with God. Elie Wiesel put it this way when describing the need for the Messiah during the Holocaust:

> When misfortune strikes some of the people of Israel, all the people are stricken at the same time. All the suffering of our people are rungs on the ladder of history. The enemy who persecutes us doesn't single out our merchants, our sages, our fools, or our poets. He who kills a Jew aims to kill all Jews. Bankers and rabbis, vagabonds and dreamers, old men and children, we are all sores on the body of Israel.
>
> This is also true of the Messiah. You regulate him to heaven, but he is here among us. You imagine that he is safe, sheltered from danger, but he has come here to be with the victims. Yes, even he, he better than anyone else, knows the sorrows that consume you; he feels the fist that smashes into your face. The darkness that engulfs us, engulfs him also. It is he, here and now, who urges you not to give way to despair. It is he who has need of you. Do not abandon him. Take pity on him. He alone is worthy of your pity. You must make sure that he is not the only one among his people to survive.[5]

Looking for God among poor people is a good place to begin in the spiritual game of hide-and-seek. The fact that the Scriptures make such a big deal out of God's love for the poor is like a hint for those of us choosing to play the game. Like a child coughing when someone who is "It" passes close by or a rattling of the bushes to draw him or her closer, the Scriptures are intended to make the game a bit easier, but not too easy. Picking up on a hint doesn't necessarily mean the game is complete. It just means one is closer. Hints, of course, are there for the taking. Some choose to use them; others would rather do all the finding without any help. It is always up to the one who is doing the looking.

It would be a mistake, however, to simply believe that the only purpose of poor people is to help provide the rest of us with a sense of focus in our searches for God. There is more to it. God wants the same thing for poor people that any parents desire for their children. All parents want their children to grow up "healthy, wealthy, and wise" without the fear of living in want or being discriminated against or without the opportunity to become as happy as possible. God wants the same thing for poor people as God wants for everyone else. This is the flip side of the coin. Poor people provide us with a hint of how to find God. On the other side, we provide people with a way to overcome poverty. You cannot have one without the other.

Notes

[1]Jim Wallis, *The Soul of Politics* (New York: New Press/Orbis Books, 1994) 149.

[2]Os Guinness, *The Gravedigger File* (Downers Grove IL: InterVarsity Press, 1983) 72.

[3]Micheal Elliott, *Partners in Grace* (Cleveland: Pilgrim Press, 1992) 20.

[4]Gustavo Gutierrez, *The Power of the Poor in History* (New York: Orbis Books, 1983) 93.

[5]Elie Wiesel, *The Legends of Our Time* (New York: Shocken Books, 1982) 59.

Chapter 6

Looking for God
in a New Age

It began sometime during the birth of the "me" generation of the 1980s. Self-help books turned into the self-help movement, which has now become the New Age movement. The conception of the movement likely began in the late 60s and early 70s when the black power movement, women's movement, gay movement, and a lot of smaller movements were founded. These trips of self-discovery for like-minded people converged in the 80s as the Age of Aquarius became a new age in which virtually every facet of human existence had a focus group and a self-help book. Society's search for spirituality, once primarily embodied through institutional religion, has increasingly become a private matter. We no longer need to attend church, or even bother with other people if we don't want to, because every nearby bookstore carries volumes on whatever we wish to explore. Should we still recognize the need to be part of a movement, we may participate in just about any type of support group imaginable.

These movements began outside churches and synagogues but were quickly adopted as necessary programs if congregations wished to remain relevant in helping people explore spiritual matters. As Os Guinness commented,

> Drop into your local secular bookstore sometime, and size up the amazing range of how-to and can-do publishing. Do people want to improve their memory, banish boredom, relax, cope with stress, overcome fears, brighten their love lives? It's all there for them, with self-awareness the dominant theme, and success, wealth, and peace of mind close behind. Then visit the

local Christian bookstore. The themes and style are precisely the same, only the gloss is different.[1]

Guinness pointed out that it all seemed to start with pop songs that were mimicked. "Jesus is the real thing" was the religious version of a Coca-Cola advertisement. "Jesus is a bridge over troubled water" was what songwriter Paul Simon meant to say. The great truths of religion were quickly reduced to commercial jingles.

The process went on to include virtually every fad introduced to society. When the dieting craze started, the Christian church quickly incorporated it into its sense of ministry. Guinness continued his assessment:

> Dieting Christian style became *Trim for Him*. Then, with the stress shifting to fitness, there came *Aerobic Praise*, *Devotion in Motion*, *Praise-R-Cise*, and the most astounding so far: the album *Firm Believer* and the slimming slogan "He must increase, but I must decrease."[2]

Afterwards, the small group movements began. Women's groups, men's groups, overeaters anonymous, undereaters anonymous, just-right-eaters anonymous, sex anonymous (I don't know if this means too much or too little), community building workshops (reach true community with strangers over a three-day weekend!), and a hundred other focus groups sprang into existence. It got to the point that people began identifying who they were by proclaiming which groups they belonged to. It was bound to happen. Groups focusing on people addicted to groups were established, and a new buzz word emerged: codependency. John Bradshaw defined it as "a dis-ease characterized by a loss of identity . . . out of touch with one's own feelings, needs, and desires."[3]

It was all a mixture of good news and bad. On the positive side, individuals were engaging in spiritual journeys, exploring the depths of themselves through personal study or group dynamics. People became overdependent on the group and quickly began trading one session for another in the never-ending search to find themselves and to maintain the goals of self-awareness, success, wealth, and peace of mind. The downside was that many forgot how to be themselves.

With the advent of cable television, the movement picked up even more steam and became increasingly diverse. There was Cher doing "info-mercials" on how to achieve happy skin and hair. Anthony Roberts told us how to unleash the power within. Robert Bly told us about Iron John, while Scott Peck taught us about love, then lies, community, and finally obtaining peace through golf. Deborah Tannen told us all we just don't understand. Susan Powter's presence was enough to captivate our attention without having to hear anything she was saying, choosing to stop the insanity by turning off the television. It was everywhere, accessible through E-mail, 1-900 phone numbers, and special newsletters. When all of this gets to be too much, we turn to the latest drug of choice: prozac.

If all this wasn't enough, a new wave of books was circulated. *The Celestine Prophecy* had the feel of an underground series, something no one would dare publish, and only the bravest seeker of spiritual awareness would obtain a copy. Of course, there were so many spiritual seekers that a major publisher picked up the book, and it rested on top of the *New York Times* bestseller list for months. *Mutant Message Down Under* took its place among those who want to feel they are engaging in spiritual guerrilla warfare.

What is so attractive about the New Age movement? The popularity of can-do and how-to books must be indicative of the need many of us have to continue exploring spiritual matters in our lives without the burden of religious institutions or boring ministers preaching sermons. We don't want religion anymore, but we do have a tremendous need to explore spirituality. The New Age movement is a way of accomplishing this.

Things We Like about the New Age

- The New Age deals with spiritual matters in a new way that is not as boring as the old way.
- The New Age is able to get all the really important spiritual truths into a 250-page book with a lot of really neat stories.
- The New Age focuses on all the positive things we like about religion without making us consider sentences that begin with "Thou shalt not."

• The New Age says most everything is o.k.
• The New Age doesn't force us to do anything other than discover who we truly are and then be that person.
• The New Age makes us feel holy without having to attend church.
• In the New Age movement we can be as involved as we want to be, and everyone will respect our space.
• In the New Age, if we quit, no one cares.
• In the New Age, everybody hugs everybody else, and only a few bother to sue someone.

There is certainly a lot to like about the New Age movement. It promises us everything without forcing us to do a whole lot except believe in a new cast of prophets, follow a different set of beliefs, and act out this faith on our own. The old ways of practicing religion are cast in doubt, with so many facets of institutional expressions of faith, utterly abandoned. All this is presented like a television commercial for a "new and improved" religion. In *The Celestine Prophecy,* James Redfield wrote:

> For half a century now, a new consciousness has been entering the human world, a new awareness that can only be called transcendent, spiritual. . . . At this moment in history we seem especially attuned to the life process itself, to those chance events that occur at just the right time and that bring forth just the right individuals to suddenly send our lives in a new and inspiring direction. Perhaps more than any other people in any other time, we intuit higher meaning in these mysterious happenings. We know that life is really about a spiritual unfolding that is personal and enchanting and magical—an unfolding that no philosophy or religion has yet fully clarified.
>
> And we know something else as well: we know that once we do understand what is happening, how to turn on this growth and keep it on, the human world will take a quantum leap into a whole new way of life, one that all of history has been struggling to achieve.
>
> All any of us have to do is suspend our doubts and distractions just long enough . . . and, miraculously, this reality can be our own.[4]

It is an exhilarating invitation to join a movement that has all the answers here and now. There is no requirement to spend a lifetime following God, selling everything one has and giving it to the poor, waiting for the Messiah, or reading the Bible. The answers are known and, if you are smart enough, you'll buy this book and join the search. And, truth be told, there is a great deal worth buying into.

The good thing about the New Age is that it often stimulates personal growth. Men begin to recognize the shadow their fathers still cast over their lives. Then, through guided self-reflection, they discover the child within, the warrior within, the lover within, the beast within, the magician within, and the king within. Women learn to affirm and appreciate the source that makes them more compassionate, giving, loving, and ultimately, more powerful than men. Couples realize they really do not understand what their mate is saying and learn to communicate in new and better ways. Many wonderful insights may be gleaned from what is being said and taught. There is no question that millions of people are better off because of New Age involvevment.

The New Age movement has also attracted many of us who have written off the religious institutions and churches that no longer hold any meaning for us. People who are bored to death by a sermon or can no longer stand the hypocrisy of the church are invited to explore their spirituality outside these settings.

The problem is: everything is too personal, and the New Age movement works only so long as it is confined to our private lives. What happens should someone decide to bring their spirituality into the public world—at work, school, or with a group of people who are not homogeneous? There is no place for personal spirituality in public places. Personal convictions are to remain personal. As Os Guinness said, "Individuals are free to build a world of their own heart's content—so long as they rock none of the boats in the real world."5 While it may change a person for the better, New Age religion does little to make the world a better place.

This is what's wrong with the New Age movement. It is too diverse, seeking to meet everyone's needs without making great demands. It seeks to change the world inside one's head, but does little for the problems in the outside world. Hunger, poverty, sickness, racism, and war are all outside the influence and power of the New Age. It is faddish, ever changing its teachings while promising a complete truth. It is commercial, egotistical, separatist, and, sometimes, downright weird, with medicine wheels, tarot cards, positive energies, and retreats that ask participants to beat on their chests and howl like wolves. It is a religion for the upper-middle class, leaving everyone else to their own devices.

Yet, there is something to this movement. A group of worn-out, hurting individuals gather for a workshop and start off being their fake, plastic selves with one another. Eventually they erupt into a chaos in which each challenges the other to be real until an emptiness settles on the room. Suddenly, the gift of community comes. There is acceptance, love, tears, happiness, and a peace no one had before.

A divorced man, shattered because his wife left and took his two daughters, loses his job and is forced to move back in with his parents at the age of thirty-five. He absentmindedly picks up *Iron John* for some reason and realizes he can rise from the ashes as the books says. He pulls himself together, accepts the fact he is divorced, finds new work and a new home, and begins building a new life.

A woman, abused by her father and unable to come to terms with what he did to her, is invited to a support group where she hears stories much like her own and finds the strength to tell her own story for the first time. As she talks, the years of suppressed feelings and emotions are released, and the healing process begins. For all the things people find wrong with the New Age movement, there is something right. Healing happens. Growth is generated. Community commences.

God is playing hide-and-seek again, touching this person and that group; dropping hints of truth, healing, community, forgiveness, and peace. Choosing unlikely prophets to deliver the message and unconventional methods to drop the hints, God lets those who are somehow in the right place or for whatever reason pick up on what is happening and know that couples can understand each other, healing can come, and the insanity can stop.

In the grand scheme of things, it drives theologians and other professional Christians crazy. We want God to be more predictable, making revelations in the same places, always communicating in the same ways. The New Age movement is too secular, too profane, and often too outlandish to be a proper way of communicating with God. The playing field is too big for traditional Christians, so they partition off whole sections of the world claiming there is no reason to look for God there because they know for certain there is only one path and one way to look. For them, God is in a box—as J. B. Phillips put it—and all of creation is not the playing field.

And yet, there is something. Many people experience the promises of religion for the first time, not in a synagogue or a church, but in a workshop, a seminar, or watching a cable television show. Many begin playing the game of hide-and-seek with God once they have been effectively summoned. Religious institutions often extend invitations in only one way. God evidently prefers a large, ever-expanding group to play with and will forever choose new people to participate in the fun at any time and in most any way.

When some children play the game of hide-and-seek, they only want their friends to play. If a new kid moves to the neighborhood, they are often slow in accepting them and will sometimes ignore the child who is standing aside watching them have fun. The child stands by the fence, obviously wanting to be invited to play, but the group merrily goes on with its closed game. Sometimes if the child stands there long enough, someone in the group may grow tired of the child and ask him or her to come on over. Many times, however, the others simply go on with their game.

God may stop the game at any time and come out of hiding long enough to invite a new person to play. God may simply stand up and extend an invitation or sneak up behind us, tap us on the shoulder, and shock us into playing. "Come on, you can play," God will shout, startling us into knowing there is a game going on when we were beginning to believe nothing was happening in the world except whatever was happening inside our heads.

If we are lucky, we understand the invitation and join in with the others. If, however, we choose to remain focused on ourselves, angry that others did not make a big deal over our presence, we remain on the sidelines wanting God all to ourselves.

Hide-and-seek is a game of surprises. The best hiding places are the ones we never think of. We have the most fun when we are completely surprised and find someone when we were on the verge of giving up.

Notes

[1]Os Guinness, *The Gravedigger File* (Downers Grove IL: InterVarsity Press, 1983) 83.

[2]Ibid., 84.

[3]John Bradshaw, *Home Coming* (New York: Bantam Books, 1990) 8.

[4]James Redfield, *The Celestine Prophecy* (Hoover AL: Satori Publishing, 1993) author's note.

[5]Guinness, 77.

Chapter 7

Looking for God in the Outdoors

Many people look for God outdoors. We like it outdoors, and many of us complain that we don't get out enough. Of course, those of us who work outdoors wish we were inside more, especially if it happens to be raining or if it's too cold or too hot. Nevertheless, most of us like it when we can spend some time traveling to a favorite outdoor destination such as the mountains or the ocean. These are times to step off the treadmills of our fast-moving lives, slow down, and, if we are lucky, do some reflecting on things we are normally too busy to consider. If there is no time to get out of town, we may simply decide to eat lunch in the park, sit on the roof at night and look at the stars, or take a walk around the block. However we do it, being outdoors reminds us we are part of the universe, and this often gets us thinking about things.

The Drifters had it right when they sang, "when this ol' world keeps on getting us down" we can "climb way up to the top of the stairs, and all our cares seem to drift out into space." "Up on the roof" we leave the rat race below and watch the stars and somehow begin thinking about things that seem more important than work, bills, fights with our kids, or deadlines we cannot possibly meet. The outdoor air cleans our heads and refreshes our souls, even if we're in the middle of a smog-congested city with the background of traffic and street noise.

Being outdoors with no particular agenda is especially good. We can meander aimlessly and take the time to see the joys of blooming flowers, sunrises, rainstorms, and blue skies. Of course, the more exotic the excursion, the more relaxed we seem to become, even if we have to rush in order to make a connecting flight. Most everyone wants to travel to the Caribbean or Grand Canyon, view the splendor of creation, and recharge their batteries. Time off at home is different. There are enough unfinished chores to keep us busy for weeks, or the routine is the same, and the reflection doesn't come as easily. It is always better to be outdoors somewhere else, although many of us are smart enough to take the Drifters' advice on a more consistent basis. There is a great deal to like about being outdoors.

Things We Like about Being Outdoors

- Being outdoors during the workday makes us feel like we're playing hooky from the job, and the same burst of excitement that hit us when we skipped school is lurking under our skin.
- Being outdoors is full of surprises. It may rain, the wind may pick up, or the sun and the moon may be shining at the same time.
- Being outdoors is believed to clear our heads, and we like it when the everyday clutter we deal with evaporates—even if just for a little while.
- Being outdoors helps put things in perspective for us. We see the vastness of the sky or the sea and are reminded we are part of the universe.
- Being outdoors reminds us we are still children inside, and, if we're certain no one is looking, we may jump or skip or sing out loud to ourselves.
- Being outdoors gives us the occasion to view the power of nature, the wind bending trees or the raging ocean attacking the rocks on shore, and we remember we are only human.
- Being outdoors gives us the occasion to see the order of the universe. Flowers grow, tall grass gently sways in the breeze, and soft summer rain cleans our face and makes us feel better.
- Being outdoors in the early morning allows us to see the rising sun, which is always one of nature's most stunning sights. This often reminds us that every day is a new chance to start over. In the same way, watching a setting sun reminds us that one day we will die.

• Being outdoors in the evening allows us to see the moon, the stars, and sounds of the universe. This often inspires in us a sense of awe and intense reflection.
• The older we get, the more we appreciate being outdoors. Because we want to feel as young as possible for as long as possible, we like to be outdoors and feel young.

In and of itself, being outdoors is serious business, especially if we choose to go out alone. If we are outdoors with friends, we seem to focus on them more by playing, talking, or simply appreciating that we are with someone else. The outdoors inspire introspection if we are by ourselves and intensity our focus if we are with another. Friendships often seem more intense outdoors. Being outdoors is one of the very best places to look for God. Somehow it makes us more attuned to godly things, even if we don't recogize God.

Charles and Linda were taking a well-deserved vacation at the beach. Their two children were staying with grandparents, so the couple was having something of a second honeymoon. It had been a tough year. Charles had a difficult time at work and was under the gun to increase productivity in his department. Linda had a new supervisor whom she considered to be sexist and had grown pessimistic about her chances for advancement. The boys had recently been promoted to a new school and were having a hard time adjusting. The Mastercard was maxed out. The tree in the front yard was dying. It was time for a break.

As they strolled down the beach one afternoon, holding hands and trying to relax, a thunderstorm built over the water. Dark clouds formed, lightning flashed, they heard thunder, and rain was visibly falling into the ocean. Charles and Linda strolled in the sunshine watching the storm in the distance.

"You know," Charles said, as they walked hand in hand, "that storm over there is kind of like our lives right now."

"What do you mean?"

"Well, a lot of stuff is going on right now, with our jobs and with the boys, but here we are. It's like that storm over there is our lives, all crazy and scary. But here we are outside of it for a little while. We called timeout so we could recharge our batteries. We're here on vacation, in the sunshine, and our lives are over there in the storm."

They walked in silence for a few moments, keeping their eyes on the clouds, before Linda spoke. "You know, it's hard to realize how crazy our lives get. If we were always aware of everything we were dealing with at the same time—lousy bosses, sick kids, the Mastercard bill—we would be insane."

"Those clouds really do look like our lives, don't they?" Charles asked.

"Thank God we stepped outside of it for a little while."

"It's funny, in a couple of days that is what we will be stepping back into."

They watched the dark bellowing clouds move closer to the beach and decided they better turn around and return to the hotel. The image of their lives hung over their heads while the storm remained suspended over the ocean.

"Do you think everything is going to work out?" Linda asked.

Charles shrugged his shoulder and seemed lost in thought. It was several moments before he answered. "Storms always die out after a while. That one will hit the shore and drive everybody inside for a little while, but then it will be gone. It's tough when it hits, and what gets you through is the knowledge it won't last."

Linda agreed. "We'll jump back into all the bad stuff in our lives knowing that it won't last."

"And we'll be better able to deal with it because we have a better perspective of everything that is going on."

They went on to spend the better part of the evening talking about how they wanted to deal with this situation and that problem. They discussed everything and began to feel they had a better handle on things. When they emerged from their hotel room the next morning, the sun was bright and the ocean calm. They sat in beach chairs and felt the warmth of the sunshine on their faces. Somehow it convinced them that life is good, in spite of their problems, and they had the ability to deal with whatever they encountered.

God likes to hide behind thunderclouds, and, while we may not always get a good look, sometimes we are able to capture the fact. What happened to Charles and Linda was not a religious experience. There were no devout words, whispers of prayer, or piety in their observations. They were merely in tune with what was happening around them, introspective enough to see things they normally miss and wise enough to take advantage of both.

There are always things that seem to get in the way and inhibit our ability to appreciate being outdoors for too long and may prevent us from finding God. Mosquitoes, for instance, always seem to land on the back of our necks and suck blood out of us at just the moment we are getting interested in something. Lightning storms creep up on us, and, because we were all taught to go inside during a lightning storm, we rush towards the nearest shelter. We sweat when it's too hot and freeze when it's too cold. Someone has allowed their dog to defecate on the exact path we happen to be walking upon.

Such things trigger other bothersome thoughts for many of us. These sudden considerations totally disrupt whatever joy we are experiencing. Try as we may, it is extremely difficult to recapture the magic of the previous moment when everything was right with the world. Our own thinking often prevents us from finding God when looking outdoors.

Things We Don't Like to Think about When We're Outdoors

- A shrinking ozone layer, the greenhouse effect, and the fact we are sweating at the moment.
- We sometimes think about pollution after we smell some strange odor we cannot identify, for instance, the smell of feet.
- Droughts, floods, hurricanes, tornadoes, or the weather in general. We would prefer to control the weather outdoors in the same way we do inside.
- Loud music from passing cars or boom boxes reminds us we really have not gotten away from it all.
- Overpopulation. It always seems that when we are alone, we bump into somebody else.
- Wild animals that attack and eat people. If we are swimming in the ocean, the theme from the movie *Jaws* plays itself in our heads, and walking through the woods convinces us that many a giant snake is behind the next tree.

- The fact that we are too out-of-shape to enjoy the walk we are taking.
- Strip mining reminds us that people really are destroying the earth.
- Empty beer cans and other trash we somehow always find.
- Toxic waste or all those movies where it creates a monster in the woods when we happen to be taking a well-worn path through a forest.

In spite of such considerations, we still have a tendency to plan the majority of our vacations so we can be outdoors. We want to be in the country with wide open farmland, rows of crops, and fish ponds. We want to stand atop the highest building and see the city lights spread out beneath the stars. We want to sail the ocean. We want to climb a mountain. Of these, most of us prefer either the mountains or the ocean. Many intense arguments start over which is the better way to appreciate the outdoors.

Some believe that mountains are the greatest thing about being outdoors. We like to see them, climb them, stand on top, and look down at the rest of the world. Others like to jump off mountains, repel them, hang glide, or simply try to stand up straight when walking down. On mountains we discover beautiful scenery, rushing creeks, towering waterfalls, and a spectacular view of the stars.

Others believe the ocean is the best place to experience being outdoors. We like to swim, sail, fish, float, jet ski, and book passage on big ships. Some like to walk beside the ocean, sit next to it, or view it from the window of the motel room. We see spectacular sunrises, sunsets, moonrises, moonsets, or incredible paths of light dancing on the nighttime water's surface. We believe the best and highest mountains are underwater, anyway, and to scale the top of them merely demands we go to the right island.

Both the mountains and the ocean are good places to start looking for God. The rules of the game remain the same, for we never can be sure what we are looking for. Many of us confuse God with nature because the things we experience outdoors are so big, so large, and so beautiful that we feel it must be God. It is just another way, however, of God playing hide-and-seek.

Certainly, many people scoff that there is no God behind a thundercloud, or anywhere else for that matter. They may be right. But that's the thing about hide-and-seek. You can never be sure. If God is the thing behind creation, then why not? Perhaps creation is one of the hints God is always dropping. Frederick Buechner said,

> Using the same materials of earth, air, fire, and water, every twenty-four hours God creates something new out of them. If you think you're seeing the same show all over again several times a week, you're crazy. Every morning you wake up to something that in all eternity never was before and never will be again. And the you that wakes up was never the same before and will never be the same again either.[1]

If we are looking in the right way, the chances of actually finding God are bound to increase.

What about the outdoors sets us on the edge of seeing things normally beyond our ability to comprehend? If we have time to let the feeling out, a sense of childlike wonder emerges. We study rainbows, looking to see if there really is something at the end. We stare at the moon and contemplate green cheese and if there really is a man looking back at us. We stroll along the beach and wonder about whales and sharks and the creatures of the deep. We lie in the grass, play in the mud, stare at the clouds in the sky, and really do stop and smell roses. We stand atop a mountain and wonder how close to heaven we are. We pick out whatever constellations we recognize in the nighttime sky and wonder how people figured out what that particular cluster of stars meant.

"You must become as a child to enter the kingdom of heaven," the Bible says. The outdoors call the child within each of us to come out to interact with the adult we try to be. The combination puts us in the same frame of mind as the writer of Psalms thousands of years ago.

> O Lord, . . . how majestic is thy name in all the earth! You have set your glory above the heavens. . . . When I look at your heavens, the work of your fingers, the moon and the stars that you have established; what are human beings that you are mindful of them, mortals that you care for them? (8:1, 3-4)

Even those of us who do not believe in God sometimes find ourselves marveling at the beauty and wonder of the world. Just for a moment, when the wind dies down and the stars are especially bright, we cock an ear towards heaven and look around to see if perhaps, just maybe, God is there. If we knew what God was supposed to look like, we would likely see something during those moments when we are expectant and prepared.

More often than not, however, instead of continuing the search, the adult takes over, and the child is suppressed. We begin to think about how silly we must look, staring at the ocean or off the top of a mountain, seriously expecting God to pop out and pat us on the back for pausing long enough to suppose something is there. We recover from such moments of insanity quickly enough to get on with our lives. While our minds quickly dart to scientific explanations of rainbows or to contemplation of what we want for dinner, our souls sigh because we begin shutting out the wonders of nature just the moment it begins communicating with us.

There is a great deal of talk these days about listening to the earth and getting back to nature. Truly, the outside world has a lot to say. We are always in need of slowing down. C. S. Lewis and J. R. R. Tolkin used to plan and take long walking journeys from their homes to wherever the destination happened to be. During these walks, each would have time to think, reflect, and see. It is interesting how both men thought such escapes to the outdoors were important. Lewis would compose books in his head if he were not trying to engage his friend in some debate. Tolkin, on the other hand, would stop and spend long moments studying trees or flowers. Both were inspired as a result of such treks. The fruits of the time spent outdoors were creations of their own worlds with books about a place called Narnia and the Shire full of hobbits.

While all of us may not be writers, having the time to mix with nature causes us to express ideas we rarely think of otherwise. We break the routine of our daily lives when we travel outdoors, and somehow the stimulation breeds new ideas and deeper thoughts. Also, the earth itself seems to be talking, and, if we have cleared our heads enough, we can sometimes hear what is being said. But most of us miss it because we do not understand a language without spoken words. Tree branches clack together. Wind brushes leaves. Water laps against the shore. All these may be ways of God saying, "Here I am." At least, that's the way it is for those of us playing the hide-and-seek game of faith. We are trying to believe things we cannot see, as the Bible puts it.

Note

[1]Frederick Buechner, *Wishful Thinking* (San Francisco: Harper & Row, 1973) 18.

Chapter 8

Looking for God at Funerals

People really *want* to find God at funerals. Someone dies and a service is quickly planned by the professional mourners employed by the funeral home to make money off someone else's grief. The deceased is dressed up as if he or she is going out for a night on the town. The mode of transportation is the finest casket the family can afford. The send-off ceremony usually takes place in a room decorated with flowers arranged in every conceivable way, soft depressing music, and well-wishers who would like to do something other than attend a funeral. If the deceased happened to be popular, we may very possibly have to stand up throughout the entire service. If we had our way, we would never attend funerals, especially our own.

Many people begin each day by pouring themselves a cup of coffee and opening the newspaper to the obituary column, which they will read thoroughly. Once finished, they breathe a sigh of relief and proclaim to anyone who may be listening that it is going to be a good day. Their own funeral is not listed. While we may be growing more accustomed to watching people die on television and still cannot help but slow down when driving past an accident to see how bad it is, funerals are more personal. Attending a funeral service demands our presence and leaves us face to face with the fact that death is a reality of life. We never can really bring ourselves to accept this, and funerals instill in us a desire to think about God. Of course, many of us dislike funerals so much we cannot engage in much reflection. There are simply too many things to not like.

Things We Don't Like about Funerals

- We are not used to sitting in the same room with a dead person.
- Sitting in the same room with a dead person reminds us that we too will die one day.
- We don't like funeral directors who dress like bankers (they deposit the body), speak too softly (making us feel even worse), and try to convey a sense of empathy that has no conviction behind it.
- Most funerals are too long, and we feel we may die from old age before they are over.
- Most ministers say the same thing at every funeral, only changing the names of those directly involved.
- There is always the chance it may be our own name the minister says, and none of us wants to think we are attending our own funeral.
- We never know what to say at funerals and are uncomfortable saying much of anything.
- The best parking places are reserved.
- We begin to wonder about what funeral directors do to dead bodies before placing them in the coffin.
- We don't like it when people express honest emotions, especially grief, and would rather remember the deceased without having to watch someone cry—it's rude.

What we seem to dislike most about funerals is the sense of being powerless and helpless in staving off death. Many of us refuse to attend funerals, claiming we would rather remember the way someone was when they were alive. In fact, we don't want to have to deal with the fact that *we are near death*. Being in the same room with a dead body is one of the ways we come face to face with death. To make matters worse, the family is sitting in reserved pews, crying softly or wailing loudly, expressing their grief for all to see and feel. At such times, we really want to find God.

Confronted with these two factors, death and grief, we become painfully aware of the absence of God. The mind becomes blank. The heart breaks. The sense of pain and loss becomes overwhelming. Those mourning ask where God is in their time of need. Those of us attending the funeral, observing what is happening around us if we are not too caught up in ourselves, ask the same question—the one C. S. Lewis posed in *A Grief Observed.*

> Meanwhile, where is God? . . . When you are happy, so happy that you have no sense of needing [God], so happy that you are tempted to feel [God's] claims upon you as an interruption, if you remember yourself and turn to [God] with gratitude and praise, you will be—or so it feels—welcomed with open arms. But go to [God] when your need is desperate, when all other help is vain, and what do you find? A door slammed in your face, and the sound of bolting and double bolting on the inside. After that, silence. You may as well turn away. The longer you wait, the more emphatic the silence will become. There are no lights in the windows. It might as well be an empty house. Was it ever inhabited? It seemed so once. And that seeming was as strong as this. What can this mean? Why is [God] so present a commander in our time of prosperity and so very absent in time of trouble?[1]

Open displays of grief and despair overwhelm us, and because we feel completely powerless to do anything, we call upon God to fix things and make them right. Why have a God if we can't have divine assistance when we want it? So we focus our attention on the fact that there are people, perhaps ourselves, who desperately need to be comforted and have their hope restored. We are aware that we have done everything we can think of to fix things—made potato salad and taken it to the house of the bereaved, sent flowers, attended the funeral—but it doesn't seem to help. At such a realization we become painfully aware of the absence of God.

The conclusion we draw, if we bother to think it through, is the same conclusion C. S. Lewis reached after the death of his wife. Faced with overwhelming grief and death, our religion lets us down. There are no divine interruptions of light and love to get us through the experience. The dead is not raised to a new life on the spot. Grief is not dissipated. Broken hearts don't immediately mend. Sorrow does not just dumbfound; it seems to linger forever.

Our expectation of religion in such times is to help us escape from the painful realities of death and grief. We want God to show up and raise the dead, just as biblical stories claimed once happened. If this is not going to be the case, then we demand an incredible sense of comfort in the fact that there is an afterlife and everyone will be happy again soon. The minister should say the right words to make everyone feel better on the spot. We want tears to stop, sorrow to cease, and a divine presence so powerful that we know—in no uncertain terms—everything will be all right. These are the things we want out of our religion. The problem is it never happens this way.

We deal with these issues in the same way we do most problems: we ignore them. We get through the service and tell ourselves that time, not God, is the great healer. Our sense of expectation is greatest when confronted with death and grief, and the things we want to happen are based on what religion has taught us. Religion has made certain promises about what God will do, and we have our own sense of how they should be done.

What We Want from God at Funerals

- We have been taught that God has raised the dead. Why can't it happen again? It would make everything instantly right again.
- We have been taught that God is a comfort in our times of sorrow. Why does it seem no one is comforted? That would make things better.
- We want God to take charge of the situation and offer immediate assurance that, in spite of the circumstance, everything is all right.
- We want tangible evidence that, in spite of death, life goes on.
- We want a sense of conviction that death is not real.
- We want our ministers to say words so wise and powerful that death makes sense.
- We want to know what is going to happen in advance, without any sense of doubt, when someone dies.
- We want to know how much time we have because we don't feel anyone has enough.
- We want our religion to pay immediate dividends when the bottom seems to drop out of our lives.

• We want light at the end of the tunnel that redirects our focus on good things instead of the bad.

We have high expectations of God and our religion when we are faced with death and grief. Unfortunately, our expectation is unrealistic. In his book *Tracks of a Fellow Struggler*, John Claypool wrote:

> The problem [is] one of expectation more than experience. [C. S. Lewis] realized he had taken certain notions of what ought to happen into that valley, and that when those specific things did not happen, his disappointment almost blinded him to what was occurring.[2]

Our religion does not give us exactly what we want during difficult times. What we want is God. What we will settle for are comfort and assurances that God is in control of the situation. Religion delivers on neither.

Many of us register this in our personal deposits of faith and end up wanting to believe what religion teaches us, but take the position of not counting on it. With God, it is another matter. We make demands on God we never make on our religion. When our demands for action are answered with silence and nothing occurs to make an immediate difference, we either write God off completely, view God as unconcerned, or get mad. C. S. Lewis considered the first two options:

> Not that I am (I think) in much danger of ceasing to believe in God. The real danger is of coming to believe such dreadful things about [God]. The conclusion I dread is not, "So there's no God after all," but "So this is what God is really like. Deceive yourself no longer."[3]

A few people take the first two positions. Most simply choose to concentrate on their own lives without continuing to look for God at funerals.

There are some, however, who have not let go of the emotions death and grief bring. They confronted God in spite of the sense of being completely overwhelmed. They resolved that if God is God, then some questions demanded answering. If they could not be answered on the spot, then they will at least be asked.

After visiting a very sick child, John Shea wrote a prayer that most of us would like to verbalize but do not allow ourselves in circumstances surrounded by despair and doubt.

No hymn of praise today.
No hand-clapping alleluia
for the all-good God
and his marvelous handiwork.
Lord,
a child has been born bad.
He gangles and twitches and shames
the undiscovered galaxies of your creation.
Why could not the hands that strung the stars
dip into that womb to bless and heal?
Please no answer from Job's Whirlwind
saying how dare I.
I dare.
Yet I know no answer comes
save that tears dry up, skin knits,
and humans love broken things.
But to you who are always making pacts
You have my word on this—
on the final day of fire
after you have stripped me (If there is breath left)
I will subpoena you to stand
in the court of human pain.[4]

Our sense of expectation is so high that when God is not "It," we grow angry, like it was a child who refused to play the game according to our rules. Some of us sulk and walk away, or scream and yell like children sometimes do, or simply refuse to play with that person anymore. In the hide-and-seek game of faith, however, too many are looking in the wrong places and not picking up on the right hints left for us. In the midst of tragic death, immeasurable sorrow, and more pain than we think we can bear, holy hints are dropped for those who can pick up on them.

The first hint we often miss is that a number of other hide-and-seekers have collected themselves together. We are wanting to come to the rescue of the hurting and the crying and are trying to figure out how to best help. Like a child who falls down, scrapes his or her knee, and sits there crying, the game is suspended while everyone comes out of hiding to attend the one who is hurting. At a funeral, we stop playing the game in order to sit at a service, hold hands with someone who is crying, cook some food and take it to the house, or send flowers. Each of these is a way of saying we love you and would do just about anything to take your grief away, but we cannot think of how to best help; so maybe just being here and doing some of these things will be enough.

We also miss a hint in the things we say and the feelings behind them. "Stop crying," a child says. "It's going to be okay." In the same way, we fumble for words that might make someone feel better; and when we speak, there is a lump in our throats. We say what is in our hearts and do so with a conviction of our own compassion and uncertainty over the hurting experience. If our own words won't come, we may quote the Scriptures hoping that someone else's words may do the trick. Like a child saying the same things his mother says to him when he is hurt, we use the words we have learned. "The light shines in the darkness, and you shall overcome it" or "Cast thy burden upon the Lord, and God shall strengthen thee."

The last hint is the most confusing. The dead body sitting in front of the room is itself one of the hints. Someone we used to play with has been taken away from us, but there was a time when we were all together, happily playing the game of life. Life itself is a gift, one that none of us asked for but that each of us share. If we have our wits about us, we also recognize that everybody else's life is a gift too—like the dead person. For a certain amount of time that person was a part of our lives—touching us, challenging us, making us angry, taking love from us, and giving love back again. In spite of the fact that a life has been taken away, it was still a gift while we had it.

This is not the way we think about things. All we see is a life cut short, like a dance stopped before the music has ended. It is always unanticipated and completely unexpected. The shock seems to consume us. We seem to forget that the game of hide-and-seek with God goes on. Holy hints are dropped all around us, but we are too preoccupied to pick up on them. God is present at most funerals. We just seem to be too busy to notice.

Sometimes when children play hide-and-seek, the one who is "It" sometimes tries too hard. He or she looks and looks, often concentrating so hard on finding that they see right past people hidden right in front of them. It is often this way at funerals. We look so hard for God that our sense of expectation is raised to an impossible level. Wanting lightning bolts, we miss the soft glow in the faces of a room full of concerned and caring people.

Notes

[1]C. S. Lewis, *A Grief Observed* (New York: Bantam Books, 1963) 4-5.

[2]John Claypool, *Tracks of a Fellow Struggler* (Waco TX: Word Books, 1974) 49.

[3]Lewis, 5.

[4]John Shea, The *Hour of the Unexpected* (Niles IL: Argue Communications, 1977) 34.

Chapter 9
Looking for God in Politicians

A lot of people don't like politicians—the President, Congress, or just about any other elected official—but this doesn't deter them from loving democracy. It's the same with religion. Many people don't care for religion—denominations, television preachers, or requirements to believe this or that—but this doesn't get in the way of a real desire to find God. Every year survey polls state that fewer of us are affiliated with a particular church, yet most of us believe in God. What is confusing is when the lines get blurred, and politicians start speaking on behalf of God.

Many frustrated people ceased looking for God in church a long time ago and began listening to politicians. It makes some sense, of course, that if our religious leaders don't know where God is, then perhaps our elected ones do. Besides, politicians are forever quoting the Bible, proclaiming traditional values that seem religious, and promising to balance the budget without raising taxes (a miracle we know only God could perform). Increasingly, we see politicians getting involved with religion and religious leaders getting involved in politics. As a result, we are more confused than ever about where to find God amidst very conflicting instructions from our leaders. When little children gather together to play hide-and-seek, there is sometimes one kid who is a bully, telling everyone how the game will be played and changing the rules to fit his or her taste. Politicians are the bullies in the hide-and-seek game of faith.

Things We Don't Like about Politicians

- Most politicians seemed to be perfectly normal human beings before they were elected to office.
- When politicians speak, it seems they are trying to convey a sense of sincerity we know is false; but we believe them anyway.
- Many politicians do a lot of things for show, for example, taking off their neckties or rolling up their shirt sleeves so we might mistake them for working women and men.
- Politicians get free mail service, but we have to pay for the bills we mail. Their mail always seems to arrive on time; ours doesn't.
- Politicians get out of paying their parking tickets; we keep ours in the glove compartment.
- We really don't know what politicians do all day, but it seems as though they never break a sweat and still make more money than we do.
- Politicians always have good reasons for why something can't be done, and it sounds good when they explain it to us, but five minutes later we're not sure what they said.
- Most politicians used to be attorneys.
- Men don't like politicians who have beautiful wives because it intimidates them. They don't like most female politicians who are more intimidating than the University of Georgia offensive line and are married to men who want to become the First Lady. (This is sexist, but it's the way a lot of people feel.)
- Politicians always seem to be running for office, taking credit for things we know they had absolutely nothing to do with, even when it is not election time.

I wonder why anyone wants to run for political office. As Lewis Grizzard wrote,

> It's expensive, it's tiring, and you have to kiss a lot of fat babies, and fat babies have a habit of drooling on you when you try to kiss them. And after you're elected, although you do have a good opportunity to become wealthy, you still have to wear a tie to work every day, people write nasty letters about you in the newspapers, and if your kid gets arrested for shoplifting

you have to deny you even know the little devil or face losing when you run for re-election.[1]

Most politicians talk about being called to public service, which is very close to how ministers describe how either their mothers or God got them to enter the ranks of professional Christians (or rabbis or religious instructors). The difference here is we're not certain who is doing the calling. Politicians never seem to explain it, and we simply figure they are masochists who like doing their thing in public.

One explanation floating around seems to make a lot of sense. Attorneys who make A's in law school go on to have careers in international law and make a tremendous amount of money. Those who make B's have careers in corporate law and make a great deal of money. Those who make C's open up successful private practices and make a lot of money. Those who make D's run for public office. Regardless of why they do it, politicians are part of our lives and want to convince us they have all the answers to life's most pressing problems, including religion.

To listen to many of them, if a particular politician has his or her way, the country will return to traditional family values, and God will be much easier to find. If the clock is turned back, there will be no drugs, crime, homelessness, or other social problems that distract us in our search for God. Regardless of the political affiliation, these politicians claim they know how to make things better. They concentrate all their attention on the playing field for the game of hide-and-seek while rarely participating in the game. They become referees and umpires by making certain patriotism and religion are so intermixed that many of us believe we must also be good Democrats or Republicans in order to find God. This is probably why so many churches have American flags beside the pulpit and patriotic songs in the hymnbook. These things have little to do with finding God, but democracy is such an easier thing to participate in than the hide-and-seek game of faith. When our candidate wins, it is a tangible thing we can see and celebrate. If that candidate has said a lot of religious things during the campaign, we believe we are closer to finding God.

Increasingly, politicians and their prophets of commentators have moved to the point of telling us what God is and what God is not. They seem to focus most on which political party God belongs to. P. J. O'Rourke stated that he only has one firm belief about the American political system:

> God is a Republican, and Santa Claus is a Democrat. God is an elderly, or at any rate, middle-aged male, a stern fellow, patriarchal rather than paternal, and a great believer in rules and regulations. He holds men strictly accountable for their actions. He has little apparent concern for the material well-being of the disadvantaged. He is politically connected, socially powerful, and holds the mortgage on literally everything in the world. God is difficult. God is unsentimental. It is very hard to get into God's heavenly country club.
>
> Santa Claus is another matter. He's cute. He's non-threatening. He's always cheerful. And he loves animals. He may know who's been naughty and who's been nice, but he never does anything about it. He gives everyone everything they want without thought of *quid pro bono*. He works hard for charities, and he's famously generous to the poor. Santa Claus is preferable to God in every way but one: There is no such thing as Santa Claus.[2]

O'Rourke has perfectly captured the message modern politicians are giving to us. The more conservative the politician, the more we are to believe he knows who God is. The more liberal the politician, the less she knows about God. The intriguing thing is: such a message works. Many of us believe the conservatives because we want to believe in God more than in Santa Claus. How else can we explain Ronald Reagan, a politician who spoke like a religious man but rarely went to church and had tremendous popularity over Jimmy Carter, a politician who didn't speak like a religious man but did attend church? There is comfort in knowing that our elected leaders have some cognition that most of us want God, and as long as they are promising us everything else under the sun to get elected, they may as well promise us God too.

In reality, politicians rarely deliver on anything they promise, especially a country closer to God. Like the playground bully who makes up his or her own rules while playing the game, politicians simply make all kinds of outrageous claims we really want to believe, even when we should know better. It has gotten to the point that many of us are more concerned about who is in the White House than we are if we find God or not. Given the choice of meeting the President or meeting God, most of us would probably opt to meet God. Besides, as Robert McAfee Brown once pointed out, "No Savior will ever sleep in the White House."

The thing to always remember about politicians and other playground bullies is this: their main concern is to protect their turf and power. They will go to most any extreme in order to remain in their positions of leadership and control. Politicians have only one primary goal: to at least keep what they have. They will risk most anything and say most everything if they believe it will help them maintain their office.

Lewis Grizzard once had a friend who ran for a local county post and lost. He told Grizzard: "It was the worse experience I ever had. Every time I told a lie, they caught me, and every time I told the truth, nobody would believe me."[3] Most of us believe that successful politicians are the ones who don't get caught when telling a lie. Even when we don't want to believe them, they say the right things; and somehow we get caught up in their words and worry about the playing field more than whether or not we find God.

While it is true that many politicians regularly attend synagogue or church and act like religious people, the fact of the matter is they believe in a higher office more than a higher power. Conversely, God doesn't seem to like hanging around the White House, Congress, governors' mansions, city halls, or other meetings of politicians. This is probably because God is aware that politicians are not really very interested in playing hide-and-seek.

To make matters even worse, some religious leaders are telling us we should focus on finding the right politicians instead of finding God. Standing in the pulpit, with a view of the American flag over their right shoulder, these ministers claim to know why God likes this politician and doesn't like that one. They seek out photo opportunities with presidential candidates more than they look for God and encourage the rest of us to follow suit. No wonder we have grown frustrated and cynical at the whole game of playing hide-and-seek with God. We would much prefer a leader who will personally tell us what to do in a time of crisis than a God who won't. God is a Republican; Santa Claus is a Democrat.

Only thing is God doesn't play the game by anyone else's rules. God can choose to be Santa Claus just as much as a Republican. Part of playing hide-and-seek is for us to figure out if God is hiding under the guise of one or the other and even acknowledging the fact that it may be neither. Politicians would prefer that we didn't come at things this way because we may become more concerned with actually finding God than we are in listening to whatever they are telling us.

One Christmas Eve, David Bradley captured the fallacy of religion and politics when he wrote these words:

> There is talk of new taxes. The decree may not be going out from Caesar Augustus, but all of the world is surely taxed, and a lot of poor Joes are putting up in stables with their pregnant wives after hauling ass to the tax collector. No mention is made of the market in frankincense or myrrh, but gold prices are up, which is bad news for the Wise Men. Worse, it seems that following stars is not as lucrative as it once was: the earth-bound explorers at the Jet Propulsion Laboratory have announced that the waning of interest in planetary exploration has forced them into doing work for the Defense Department. The lame-duck session (aren't they all) of which Congress this is (does it matter?) has accomplished exactly what you would expect from a quacking cripple—although in the spirit of the season they have passed another continuing resolution, so that, like the rest of America, they can deal with the bills of Yuletide spending until January. But their Christmas spirit is outdone by that Jolly Fellow in the White House, who, taking his cue from both religious and secular myths, has decided to rename the most powerful engine of destruction ever designed . . . the Peacekeeper, has wrapped up economic depression in a nice bow and called it a period of consolidation.[4]

We often remind ourselves that politics and religion don't mix, but we still seem comfortable with it in our daily lives. Ministers bomb abortion clinics while they advocate the death penalty. Civil rights leaders protest inequality in the workplace, but preach before a congregation comprised of one-color people. We want the separation of church and state to continue, but scream bloody murder if a congregation's nonprofit tax status is threatened. Saint Paul admonished us to "be perfect as God is perfect," but because we don't want to have to live up to such standards, we elect people to do it for us and take fiendish delight when the press reports they are not perfect after all.

All the while God continues to play hide-and-seek, occasionally making a political appearance just to keep us honest, but, more often than not, keeping it simple and personal. After elections are over and our candidates have lost by an overwhelming margin, we sometimes get to the point that all we can do is call upon God. When it comes to politics, we get so hung up on winning—as though the future of the world depended on our candidate or not. In the face of such defeats, we end up having to acknowledge that life goes on. The game of hide-and-seek goes on too; and, if we are not too depressed over the fact that our candidate lost or too angry over the majority of idiots who voted against him or her, we pull out the last straw. The only words the politicians can say are those that might endear them to voters the next time around. When all is lost, we look for God.

It is hard not to imagine that God is pretty ticked off that we would wait until our political alternatives are exhausted before turning our attention that way, but this doesn't seem to be God's way of doing things. When the election has been lost and our politicians have left us wanting, it seems to be one of the times God passes close by and drops a hint. If we are smart enough to catch it, and not too devastated over whatever is happening politically, we will realize that we still have hope that everything will work out regardless of who was elected. This is God's way of saying, "Here I am. Forget all that other stuff, and let's play!"

Notes

[1]Lewis Grizzard, *When My Love Returns from the Ladies Room Will I Be Too Old to Care* (New York: Villard Books, 1987) 233.

[2]P. J. O'Rourke, *Parliament of Whores* (New York: Vintage Books, 1991) xx.

[3]Grizzard, 234.

[4]David Bradley, "Christmas Eve," *While Someone Else Is Eating*, ed. Earl Shorris (Garden City NY: Anchor Press, 1984) 179-80.

Chapter 10
Looking for God in All the Wrong Places

You cannot play hide-and-seek without spending a great deal of time looking in the wrong places. It is simply part of the game to go where you think people ought to be hiding only to discover they are not really there, having picked a place we would never have thought of and forcing us to keep looking. Much of hide-and-seek is looking in the wrong places. This does not impede us from continuing the game in spite of numerous failures before we finally are successful in our search.

It is the same when playing hide-and-seek with God. We spend most of the time looking in the wrong places. We begin searching in the most obvious places that only the worse hide-and-seek players would choose. Starting in church we find sometimes decent music, choirs accompanied on tape (religious MTV live), and, hopefully, a not-too-dull sermon. We listen to the minister, picking up our ears ever so slightly, in hopes that something will be said to help us find God. We volunteer and work with the poor, the sick, and the hurting in hopes that God will also show up and work beside us. We read whatever book promises deliverance, take long contemplative walks, and wish against all reality that God will pop out of nowhere. We even get to the point that we actually listen to rather absurd promises from politicans. It gets very frustrating when we do all this looking and never seem to discover where God is hiding.

Even more frustrating, we never seem to realize we are looking in the wrong places. We are persuaded we are right. So we continue looking for God in all kinds of wrong places and wrong ways.

Many of us look for God on television. After all, we have cable access to hundreds of channels, many of which are religious. There is always some big-haired man or woman talking about how to find God. They ask us to do little more than sit on the sofa and listen to what they are telling us. Some go so far as to ask us to pray. Most have an army of operators staffing an elaborate telephone system so we can immediately get through should we decide to call. These operators always look very busy, but the big-haired host never offers us instructions on what to do should we get a busy signal; so there is always the suspicion that they are merely pretending they are talking to someone on the phone. Normally the host will ask us to write a check or use our Mastercard to make a contribution. Looking for God on television only gives us the illusion that we are active in our search. In reality, we are like the child who would rather watch cartoons than go outside and play.

Looking for God in rich people is also very appealing. Many clergy are fond of claiming that God blesses people by making them prosperous, and, because we could always use extra money, it is an easy decision to spend some time investigating their theory. We end up becoming so preoccupied with what we are wearing, whether or not we have made a good impression, or how much money we have in the bank that we don't look for God in any of the good hiding places for fear of getting dirty. Looking for God with the rich is like joining a clique of kids who think they are too good to lower themselves to playing hide-and-seek.

Many of us would rather do it all by ourselves and take the John Wayne approach to finding God. We don't need any help from anybody. So we spend a great deal of time doing what we want and never hear about good hiding places from other people. We don't pick up hints from other people who are looking for God. We make up our version of what God must look like and convince ourselves that what we believe is reality. Should we grow frustrated and discouraged—and we will—there is no one to offer us any encouragement, and we end up quitting the game. Looking for God by ourselves is like the kid who would rather play with an imaginary friend than with real people.

Likewise, looking for God by subscribing to home study courses, attending religious seminars, or even enrolling in a seminary has little to do with the hide-and-seek game of faith and even less to do with finding God. We spend some money and feel we are accomplishing something with each passing grade and each completed course. We end up getting accredited or obtaining a degree, but we don't find God. Taking a course means we become certified hide-and-seek players regardless of whether or not we actually play. Looking for God by enrolling in a class is like the child who would rather stay inside and do his or her homework than go outside and play. We may complete, even publish, a thesis on playing hide-and-seek, but we never personally find God.

On the other extreme are those who look for God by doing a lot of different things to help others. We agree to work at a soup kitchen, become a "buddy" to someone with AIDS, volunteer to work with children, or do any number of good deeds. Many wonderful things happen, and we feel good about ourselves for doing the deeds, but we still may not find God. It can become very difficult because, while the poor are certainly people God likes to hang around, there is danger if we come to believe we are of such importance that nothing happens without us. We can grow so absorbed in our own sense of self-importance that the poor become frustrated and angry. Finding God is no longer the purpose of the game, and helping the poor is like a juggler who is throwing things up and catching them as quickly as possible. It takes all our focus and energy to continue, and we wouldn't see God if we were slapped in the face.

Doing good deeds is one of the ways we ask God to find us by calling attention to ourselves. It is a way we convince ourselves we are playing the game when we are actually doing something else. Looking for God by doing all kinds of good deeds is like the kid who always wants to play a game other than hide-and-seek, regardless of what the majority wishes.

Some of us surround ourselves with religious things. Our homes are decorated with icons, religious posters, and other knick-knacks proclaiming the greatness of God. We own stacks of religious compact discs and actually watch to see if our favorite contemporary religious singer wins a Grammy award. Our book-cases are filled with theological books and commentaries, and we usually own several different translations of the Bible. While we have made a lot of vendors happy because we purchased so many wares, we haven't found God. Looking for God by surrounding ourselves with spiritual things is like the kid who covers the walls of his or her room with posters of great hide-and-seek players but who never actually plays the game.

Others of us look for God by joining a group that impresses us with what they say and do. We bond with those who have an attractive way of playing hide-and-seek. On the positive side, this allows the opportunity to meet many new friends. On the negative side, it is often separatist, and the group members feel they are better than everyone else. Looking for God by joining a particular group or cult is like the small group of children who always wanted to play their own game without inviting anyone else to play. After a while, they know each other so well no one can successfully hide from anyone else. Each is intimately familiar with the places the others hide. So they quit playing the game and go on to do other things.

Many of us are even more separatist than this and look for God by locking ourselves in a closet to pray, read, sing, or do a bunch of other things we are under the impression God likes. We don't feel that anyone else is necessary in our games of faith. We think God will be so impressed with our individual dedication and effort that surely we will be found without hesitation. Unfortunately, we end up playing hide-and-seek by ourselves, which is a very hard thing to do. Looking for God by yourself probably means no one else is playing the game with you, including God.

A few really weird ones among us look for God by denying ourselves the things we enjoy most in life. We won't wear new clothes, listen to music, eat certain foods, or go to places that look like they might be fun. We look for God by making ourselves stick out like a sore thumb. Obviously, this is a bad way to play the game of hide-and-seek, and God is good enough a player to know that.

In playing the hide-and-seek game of faith, we will look for God in the wrong places. A successful game means we will not continue to look in them, however. Looking for God means we are willing to be surprised at what we find, smart enough to pick up on the hints dropped all around us, and brave enough to go looking wherever our search takes us. There is always the possibility we will spend time looking in the wrong places, but after a while we will get good enough at the game so we will not spend all our time doing it.

Ways to Tell If You're Looking for God in the Wrong Places

- if mass gatherings of people are involved
- if elaborate theatrical productions with spotlights, elegantly dressed professionals, and egotistical people are involved
- if a candidate for political office is seated at the speaker's table or is standing behind the podium
- if the primary concern is the budget
- if you find yourself surrounded by people who are absolutely convinced beyond a shadow of a doubt that they know where God is and promise to show you
- if you find yourself as part of a homogeneous group where everyone more or less looks alike, makes approximately the same amount of money, and has the same education level
- if race, background, or sexual preference matter
- if what you wear matters
- if publicity is a primary concern
- if no spontaneity is involved

Of course, there are many who claim God can certainly be found in such places—and God may certainly show up anywhere or at any time. Ministers of really big churches, for example, will take issue with these tips and will likely go out of their way to prove them incorrect. It goes without saying that politicians won't like them. In most instances, however, they can prove to be useful in helping to prevent us from looking in all the wrong places.

They also provide a wealth of hints as to what types of places God is most likely to be found. God likes places where there is intimacy, simplicity, an honest (or no) agenda, not too much structure, the ability to admit ignorance, diversity, acceptance, and flexibility.

Unfortunately, these are things most of us can only take in small doses and have a tendency to shy away from. They prove to be too much of a challenge for us. We would rather not place ourselves in a position where we have to be intimate. We want organization in our lives. We always seem to have an agenda. It is painful for us to admit our ignorance. We easily grow uncomfortable with people who are different from us. It is hard to accept new ideas. We prefer structure. It seems we naturally recoil from the places God is most likely to be.

There is an underlying reason for this. Most of us do not like change, and such things mean either we change or those around us change. There are a lot of wonderful stories about God and change. Abram's name was changed to Abraham when he went off searching for the Promised Land. Moses changed when he left the pharaoh's house and became the spiritual leader of a group of freedom fighters. Elijah was changed when he followed God into a whirlwind. A dirty, naked madman, said to have been possessed with demons, changed when he talked with Jesus one afternoon and was found clothed and in his right mind. Buddha was changed after he sat underneath a tree one day. Being close to God means changing.

Yet most of us detest change. We don't want it. We want things to remain the way they are. We do not like it one bit when the world seems to be changing around us all the time. Often we have just gotten used to the way things are when they change again. Friends move away. Children grow older. Old leaders die, and new ones take their place. Why can't things stay the way we like them?

Worse than this is when we are forced to change. For most of us, change is always forced. If we had our way, things would stay the same. We stay away from the things that might force change upon us. If we are intimate with someone else, we will likely be challenged to face our own faults and then be confronted with the fact we should do something about them. Without our agendas, we would risk being manipulated by someone else's. A lack of structure is the same as no sense of order, and we demand to know what to expect and when. To accept people who are different from us means to take their ideas and beliefs seriously, and this would certainly mean changing the way we are accustomed to looking at things. While there is little question we want to find God, we have a tremendous amount of fear concerning what we might be forced to go through in order to succeed.

The sad fact is we cannot find God without experiencing significant change in our lives. As a matter of fact, if we claim to have found God but have not experienced enormous changes in our lives, then it is not likely we have found God. On the other hand, if we are experiencing changes for the good, we probably have found God even if we do not recognize it as such. An alcoholic stops drinking, finds a new job, and remarries. A mother leaves the streets, places her children in school, and returns to school herself, resolved to never again experience homelessness. A successful businessman finds purpose and meaning in his life after donating some time and money to a children's hospital. A teenage girl who has anorexia finds healing through the concern expressed by friends. In each instance, change occurs for the better.

Again, the thing about God and change that confuses us is our own sense of expectation. We wouldn't mind change so much if God would slap us beside the head, get our full attention, and do the changing for us. This is often the point we get out of stories about Moses and madmen filled with demons. Our attitude is that if God wanted us to change, then God would change us. Unfortunately, it doesn't work this way. Change, like hide-and-seek, is a process. As Allen Willis said, "The sequence is suffering, insight, will, action, change."[1] Finding God means looking in the places that will probably change us.

But isn't that one of the points of the game? When children go looking for their hidden mates, aren't they trying to change things so that no one is hidden? They start the game with the determination they will change what is hidden into what is found. This is the way it is in the hide-and-seek game of faith. The way we understand the present is determined by the desire we have for the future.[2] It can be slow—change most often is—but our resolve to keep playing the game keeps us active, looking here and there, until we find God. The whole point is we keep playing the game until that which is hidden has been revealed.

Notes

[1]Allen Willis, *How People Change* (San Francisco: Harper/ Colophon Books, 1973) 102.
 [2]Ibid., 115.

Chapter 11
Finding God

Finding is the best part about playing hide-and-seek. Each of us can likely recall a time when we were "It." Everyone was well-hidden, and we were looking everywhere we could think of but to no avail. Then unexpectedly, the rustling of a bush caught our eyes or we heard someone whisper, and a rush of excitement shot through our body as we inched closer to the site. Anticipation built as we stepped closer and closer. If we were wrong, and no one was hidden there, disappointment hit. If the game had been going on for some time, frustration or even anger could well up inside. But if we were right, hidden friends saw us coming, leaped out of the bushes, surprised us, and ran towards home base before we could tag them. Pushing ourselves to run faster, the chase was on. Determined to catch them, so we could feel the relief of not being "It" anymore, we pushed ourselves harder, slowly pulling closer until we could reach out and touch one and then another until all were tagged.

Afterwards, there would be laughter and relief, joy and surprise, touching and celebration. Everyone would fall all over one another, happy the game had ended. It was a moment of perfect contentment with the world. It may have been raining somewhere else, and we might have had tons of homework waiting, but for the moment, life was complete. If we could have thought of it—although we were having too much fun to do so—we would have recognized that life was perfect at such moments.

If you are like me, it is not so much the specific games you recall, but the incredible feelings of the game. I do not think these are romanticized memories of childhood. The feelings were intense and real. What we remember is a time of happiness. Leo Buscaglio expressed the sentiment well:

> Happiness is always a byproduct of some feeling or action.
> Even knowing this, there are many of us who spend our lives
> frantically looking for happiness, constantly in mad pursuit of
> joy.[1]

It was not so much the mechanics of the game, but the emotional
byproducts we can still remember.

When we as adults are asked to describe hide-and-seek to
someone who has never played, we find it difficult and may even
feel silly at the simplicity of a game that so totally engrossed us.
"Well," we might begin, "someone is 'It,' and he or she closes their
eyes and counts while everyone else hides. When finished counting, the person who is 'It' starts looking around for everyone until
they are found. That's pretty much all there is to the game."

But that is *not* all there is to it. The mechanics of the game have
been explained, but the experience of hide-and-seek would be lost
upon the listener. The unexpected happened. We were excited.
Anticipation was intense. The joy of finding someone was overwhelming. The disappointment felt when we could not find
someone was crushing. The anger over someone hiding too well
was all consuming. The happiness of finding everyone was enough
to make us giddy. We felt all these things while playing, completely
in touch with our emotions. We were content with who we were and
what we were doing. Playing the game was the most important
thing in our lives.

Then we grew up and quit playing hide-and-seek. "When I was
a child, I spoke as a child and thought as a child," the Bible says,
"but when I became an adult, I put away childish things." In another
place though, the Bible states, "Unless you become as a child, you
cannot enter the kingdom of God." It's just like the Bible to keep us
confused about such things. As we grow up, we cease looking at
life as a gift and a game. Instead, as adults we begin to view it as
something to own and control. We demand to know answers and not
wrestle with questions. We want happiness without despair and
understanding without struggle. We want to know where God is and
take solace in that knowledge. We grow tired of playing games and
want to find God now—or we quit.

Yet the Bible is right. While the paradox seems obvious, the truth is found between the two verses. As we grow, we put away many childish things. As we mature, we become capable of assuming more responsibility and increased knowledge. This takes the place of childish immaturity and ignorance. But some elements of childhood should be retained as we become adults. The enthusiasm for life and the appreciation of the moment are childhood qualities paramount in a search for God. To succeed in the hide-and-seek game of faith, adults must regain these childhood qualities.

God cannot be separated from the elements of the game. Finding God carries with it the same emotions—the acute sense of life and purpose—of children playing hide-and-seek. A good game of hide-and-seek invokes the same heartfelt passions—for example, a child's curiosity, frustration, joy, surprise, anticipation, anger, and laughter—as those involved in finding God. The only difference is that in a children's game the stakes are higher for adults. We are not looking to find another child; we are looking to find God.

Often adults make the mistake of thinking it is something else. Of course, our sense of expectation is always so high, and we look for an old man holding lightning bolts or riding a cloud down from the sky. We should be looking for something else. Always unconventional in the presentation, God revealed is never what we expect. In spite of all the false prophets, many experienced hide-and-seekers have described their experiences of finding God. The rest of us would do well to learn from them.

Elie Wiesel described a conversation in a Nazi concentration camp in which Jews wondered aloud where the Messiah was and how he could allow such a place to exist. In response, one addressed the others:

> This is true of the Messiah. You regulate him to the heavens, but he is here among us. You imagine that he is safe, sheltered from danger, but he has come to be with the victims. Yes, even he, he better than anyone, knows the sorrows that consume you, he feels the fist that smashes into your face. The darkness that engulfs us engulfs him also. It is he, here and now, who urges you not to give way to despair.[2]

Of course, they wanted a mighty warrior of a God who would deliver them from their sufferings and vanquish the Nazis. They were surprised to hear they were getting a God who silently suffered beside them, quietly encouraging them not to give way to despair.

After Jesus was crucified, Mary Magdalene and some other women went to his tomb to place flowers on the grave. When they arrived, the grave was open. Jesus' body wasn't there. Mary looked around for someone so she could determine what had happened. She found the gardener and asked him. After a few moments, she realized she was talking to Jesus himself.

> The resurrected Jesus is not in flowing white robes with face aglow; the living Christ is barefoot, dressed in work clothes, wearing a straw hat with dirt under his fingernails. Not even his closest followers were prepared for that! Even in his resurrection Jesus was not acting the way he was supposed to. And the Savior is still refusing to sit on the throne in heaven.[3]

When playing hide-and-seek with God, we should not spend so much time looking up to the heavens but pay more attention to the things going on around us.

In his excellent novel *The Clowns of God*,[4] Morris West has God explaining divine presence in a little retarded girl left to remind the rest of us of purity. Walter Wangerin says God is a rag man, wandering the streets at night, pushing a cart of discarded clothes, and taking on the hurts and pains of everyone he encounters. Graham Greene has a drunken whiskey priest experience a moment so godly that all the power and glory of heaven are his for a moment. On and on the prophets of our time write of God popping up here and there, always surprising us in the revelation and catching us completely off guard.

But these are only books, you claim, and everyone's not a reader. Besides, God cannot be found in a book. Yes, this is true, but some books can provide hints. In each description, the range of human emotions is pushed to the limit. It seems that ordinary women and men feel everything they are capable of at the same instant. God is in the feeling.

Again we must regain our childhood abilities for hide-and-seek. At the moment we were the most alive—looking for others, intense in the search, finding them, celebrating what was revealed, falling all over each other in joy and laughter—we were closest to success. God is whatever exists between you and me. That experience holds us together. God is the source of strength that allows us to keep playing the game long after we are ready to throw in the towel and quit. God is the wealth of glorious power that fosters determination, righteous anger, forgiveness, and joy. God is the source pushing us to continue to love when we are angry. God persuades us to forgive when we swore we would never forget. God is where laughter comes from when we didn't think we would ever be able to laugh again. God is that which gives life and holds us together, playing the game of life even when we are ready to give up.

John F. Smith said,

> The presence of God is in the events of history and in the events of our personal lives—in events as much as in a relationship . . . we know his resurrection when we know [God's] presence in the events of our own history.[5]

God is not a thing to be found, but feelings to be experienced and lived. This is certainly contrary to what most of us are looking for. Our search is for some deity in control of world events. Well, yes, in a way this is what we are looking for but not in the way we think. God is revealed in the emotions behind history. This is not the history recorded in books, but that of our individual and collective lives. God is the thing behind history on a small scale. God comes out of hiding most every day to each of us, but we are too busy looking for something else to appreciate the revelation. How does God come out of hiding?

Times When God Comes Out of Hiding

• A happenstance meeting of two individuals leads to a lifelong friendship that sustains one another throughout their lives. God caused the meeting and was involved in the introductions.

- A divorced couple resolves to continue as friends, placing their children first and continuing to work as a parental team instead of sparing adversaries. God kept two individuals focused on the children they berthed.
- A mother is determined to leave the streets and somehow better herself, find a job when she would prefer to wallow in self-pity, help her children with their homework, and pull the family out of homelessness. God is the silent friend who encourages such determination.
- Two friends have gone months, perhaps years, without talking. They suddenly find themselves together, and it is as if they have never been apart. Picking up where they left off, the two share their unique struggles and what they have learned in the time apart. Each is better because of it. God is the relationship the two discovered they still retained.
- A person somehow knows that something is wrong with a friend 250 miles away. She is not certain of the reason, but picking up the phone she makes a call to ask about it. She discovers she was right. God is the intuition that led to the discovery.
- A wife forgives her husband after she found him to be unfaithful, and the husband forgives himself so the marriage is repaired. God is the motivation behind forgiveness.
- A woman packs up her things and flees with her children from an abusive husband. God is the conviction that gave her the courage to protect the ones she loves.
- A man acknowledges that love is different for him. He begins to live the life given to him, being nothing other than who he is, and no longer trying to be what society wants him to be. God is the strength behind admitting the reality of life.
- Two parents are devastated at the death of a child. Life seems to lose all meaning for them. As time passes, however, they find that life carries on. As they live, hope and laughter return to their home. God is the desire to pick up and carry on with life after a child, when the very last thing a parent would want or expect is to carry on at all.
- An old man, bedridden for months and unable to see or speak intelligently, cared for by people too old or busy to care for him,

sits up in bed when asked what he wants. Breaking out in song, the voice clear and distinct, he sings the words to an old hymn: "Coming Home, Coming Home, Lord, I'm coming home." God is the power to sit up and sing in the face of death.

God is the power behind life and love. God is the source of the joy and frustration, anger and happiness, resolve and forgiveness we feel every day. God is in the whole game of life itself. God is not something we should look for so much as something we should experience. In the hide-and-seek game of faith, these are the things we should look for.

Ways that God Comes out of Hiding

- when someone offers unexpected forgiveness not deserved or anticipated
- when two people meet and both immediately like the other and a new friendship bursts into their lives
- when the unexpected opportunity to be kind to someone confronts us and we respond accordingly
- when we are motivated to stop the normal routine in our lives and discover something new
- when we are moved to laugh, especially after we thought we would never see anything humorous about a particular situation again
- when we find ourselves in a hopeless situation and discover that we are hoping anyway
- when we are faced with burdens that feel as though the weight of the world is on our shoulders and we will not possibly be able to carry on, but we find that we are carrying on anyway
- when we don't feel good about ourselves and cannot reason why anyone would want us to be their friends, but are confronted with people who resolve to be our friends regardless of how we feel
- when a child says or does something that strikes us as being so profound that we decide to remember it as an important lesson in our lives
- when we wake up each morning and have some understanding of this being a chance to start our lives completely over

Each of these revelations is unexpected, coming as a surprise, sometimes knocking us off our feet, always filling us with a renewed sense of life and purpose we did not have only a few seconds earlier. This is finding God in our lives. Finding is always outside of the routine and carries a shock because it is so unexpected. God revealed is also quite simple. This is why we miss so many chances to see. When it comes to God, we are determined that it will always be a very dramatic event when, in fact, it is the simple miracles of everyday life that are waiting to be found. Remember, God doesn't feel that anyone must be impressed.

Children are enamored with life's simplicities. They can be enthralled with a rainbow or a collection of rocks. Children love others unconditionally. They have no problem accepting this as they are without wishing they are different. Children seem the wonder behind most everything. Adults, however, have put away such childish things. Grown-up knowledge and maturity demand something other than simplicity. In our search for God, we adults often determine what we want to find and then miss what we were looking for. Such an approach always seems to mess us up. Because we fail to recognize God in the things around us and happening to us, we miss the find and don't even know it.

An old friend does something to hurt us, and we fleetingly think about forgiveness—moving on as if it were no big deal—but instead we allow the hurt and anger to prevail. The friendship erupts into an explosion of accusations and anger. As a result, it does not survive. God was present during the argument, and we had the opportunity for the find in the midst of the situation. At that point when the hurt and anger began to prevail, we started growing colder and colder as children sometimes warn. The friendship is lost. God causes friendships to be born and keeps them together, but we grow colder, moving further from God, when we allow them to die.

During such moments, our primary concern is not finding God but remaining in control. We still want things to be the way we want rather than accepting things for what they are. A friend unexpectedly drops by and asks what is wrong. Instead of sharing what is bothering us, we rationalize that we do not want to share the reality of our emotions. Determined that we should be able to work things out alone, we don't want to be a burden to anyone. So the friend leaves. At the moment when we resolved to handle things by ourselves, we grew colder and missed God in the moment.

Or we could have been the friend who allowed us to handle things when encouragement and help were needed. It could have been that we felt we had our own problems and didn't need another's burden, so the encounter remained superficial. At the moment when it was determined that help would not be given or received, God was missed.

Someone is sick with a strange disease, and we are afraid he may die. Not knowing what to say or do, we visit the hospital and sit with the family. "How could God allow such a thing to happen?" We do our best to think of something to say and to justify the reality of pain. We presume to speak for God. Mumbling something about it being God's will, we minimize the reality of the love and emotions in the room. When we presumed to take God's place, we grew colder. Because God was present sitting between you and your friend, causing you to sit there in the first place, there was no need to have said anything. The only thing needed was to acknowledge God's presence.

Each moment of our lives is pregnant with the possibility of recognizing God in the everyday encounters with things, events, and people. Because we are looking for a tangible expression of God, we miss what we are searching. To successfully find God, we must learn to see things the way God sees them. Michel Quoist expressed it well:

> If we knew how to look at life through God's eyes, we would see it as innumerable tokens of the love of the Creator seeking the love of his creatures. [We have been] put into this world, not to walk through it with lowered eyes, but to search for [God] through things, events, people. Everything must reveal God to us.[6]

Each encounter of our lives is pregnant with the possibility of finding God. We must simply resolve to remain focused on how God likes to be revealed.

God is the thing in-between. Hints are dropped all around us. In the hide-and-seek game of faith we should not try to win so much, but rather be the ones who point God out to everyone else. To find God is to be able to recognize the feelings and emotions between ourselves and others. When these feelings are intense and very strong, then God is present. The experiences are the primary parts of the game.

Looking for physical manifestations of God in our lives is to miss the boat. God doesn't seem to be into anthrophomoric express-ions of the divine. It is not what we want; it is reality. To succeed in our search is to recognize that God seems to prefer delegating a great deal of communication. In fact, God speaks loud and clear through other people and things.

> Unfortunately, most of us would rather be addressed directly, even though God is obviously more comfortable delegating joyous exclamations or tear-stained shoulders to others.[7]

Hide-and-seek success is the result of staying focused on what we are looking for. Failure is getting sidetracked into looking for some-thing else.

To help stay focused, there are several things to keep in mind about God in the hide-and-seek game of faith. First, God likes to delegate, so we must listen for the message rather than concentrat-ing on the messenger. Hearing what is said and feeling the emotions are the important things. Second, God is comfortable enough not to have to make a grand entrance. Discovery is often in the humdrum everyday activities of our lives. Third, God is polite enough to let other people do all the talking even when they are wrong. This is true even when God wants to say something. If we are doing all the talking, then we can't be listening at the same time. Finally, God doesn't seem to prefer the spoken word anymore. The emotions and feelings behind words are the modern-day language of God.

All of life is the playground. Hints are dropped around us most every moment of every day. We must train ourselves, of course, to catch and explore them. If we do, God will certainly be found. Once we know what we are looking for, success is almost certain. So what are you waiting for? Go out and play! God is ready to be found!

Notes

[1]Leo Buscaglia, *Loving Each Other* (Thorofare NJ: Slack Publishing, 1984) 114

[2]Elie Wiesel, *The Legends of Our Time* (New York: Shocken Books, 1982) 59.

[3]Micheal Elliott, *Community of the Abandoned* (New York: Crossroads/Continuum, 1991) 21.

[4]Morris West, *The Clowns of God* (New York: St. Martin's Press).

[5]John F. Smith, *The Bush Still Burns* (Kansas City: Sheed Andrews and McMeel, Inc., 1978) 10.

[6]Michel Quoist, *Prayers* (New York: Avon Books, 1963) 17.

[7]Micheal Elliott, *Partners in Grace* (Cleveland: Pilgrim Press, 1992) 17.